# OXFORD
## *Children's Book of the*
# 20th
# CENTURY

*A concise guide to a century
of contrast and change*

Stewart Ross

# OXFORD UNIVERSITY PRESS

Oxford University Press, New York

Oxford    New York
Athens    Auckland    Bangkok    Bogotá    Buenos Aires    Calcutta
Cape Town    Chennai    Dar es Salaam    Delhi    Florence    Hong Kong    Istanbul
Karachi    Kuala Lumpur    Madrid    Melbourne    Mexico City    Mumbai
Nairobi    Paris    São Paulo    Singapore    Taipei    Tokyo    Toronto    Warsaw
and associated companies in
Berlin    Ibadan

Published by Oxford University Press, Inc.,
198 Madison Avenue, New York, New York 10016

First published 1998

Library of Congress Cataloging-in-Publication Data

Ross, Stewart.
    Oxford children's book of the 20th century: a short guide to the
great events of the century / Stewart Ross.
        p.    cm.
    Includes index.
    Summary: Provides a conceptual overview of the twentieth century,
depicting large ideas such as "art" or "cooperation" by focusing on
particular people, innovations, or events.
    1. History, Modern--20th century--Juvenile literature.
[1. History, Modern--20th century.]    I. Title.
D422.R67    1998
909.82--dc21                                            98-31233
                                                       CIP    AC


ISBN 0-19-521488-9

1  3  5  7  9  10  8  6  4  2

Designed by Keith Shaw, Threefold Design
Printed in Belgium

# CONTENTS

# THE AMAZING CENTURY

The 20th century saw human beings at their best and their worst: wonderfully creative and compassionate, but also destructive and cruel. This made it a period of confusion, contrast, and almost unbelievable change.

▶ One world, one meal: from Beijing to Boston, in the second half of the century the burger was the planet's favorite food.

## NEW FRONTIERS, NEW LIFESTYLES

The political map of the world was drawn and redrawn. Empires came and went. Dozens of new countries appeared. Europe twice tore itself apart, then rebuilt itself into the European Union. China and Russia went through long years of trouble. The United States matured into the richest and most powerful country in the world.

Entertainment and sports grew into billion-dollar industries. In some parts of the world religious beliefs fell away, in others they found a new lease on life. Some strange things happened, too: we lived and worked in lofty glass towers; time-saving machines made us busier than ever; we invented teenagers; we preserved our past but longed to be modern; film stars were more famous than kings.

## ALL CHANGE!

The biggest change was in the number of people living on Earth. The world's population doubled in the first 60 years of the century, then doubled again over the next 40 years. This had many serious effects. The most important were the growth of cities, the need for more food, and damage to the natural environment.

Science and technology also changed at great speed. In 1903, for example, the Wright brothers made the first flying machine. Twenty years later airplanes were crossing the oceans, and 40 years after that astronauts were soaring into space. Automobiles were rare machines in 1900. A hundred years later they had become part of many people's everyday lives. Doctors discovered the basic materials of life and treatments for most known diseases. A vast number of gadgets and man-made materials transformed home life in better-off countries. From the 1960s onwards, air travel, satellite TV, and computers made everyone neighbors.

◀ At the heart of the communications revolution. Satellites orbiting Earth made it possible to relay TV programs, telephone conversations, faxes, and emails across the world in seconds.

◄ Nazis on parade. While democratic countries worked for individual rights, fascist (Nazi) countries urged people mindlessly to follow their leader.

## MISERY AND HOPE

The century began with 10 quite peaceful years. Then came 40 years of terrible wars and serious economic problems. There were revolutions and other violent outbreaks, too. Finally, scientists invented weapons capable of destroying the entire human race. It was difficult to be hopeful about the future.

Fortunately, the second half of the century turned out somewhat better than the first. There were wars, but no one used nuclear weapons, and there was no fighting on the same scale as the world wars. Powerful countries gradually learned to live together in peace. Democracy and human rights spread slowly through a new world of nations. The rich countries got richer still, but they polluted the environment and did not share their wealth widely.

► Too terrible to use. Although nuclear weapons could destroy civilization, fear of using them helped to prevent a third world war.

## GLOOMY OR CHEERFUL?

It is possible to take two very different views of the century.

One is dark and gloomy. It points to the awful wars and the attempts to wipe out whole races. These brought pain and suffering on a scale never seen before. Cruel tyrants added to the unhappiness. So did famine and the heart-breaking poverty found in huge cities. To make matters worse, we failed to care for the future health of our planet.

The second view is more cheerful. It praises the spectacular advances in medicine, technology, and communications. The work for peace and co-operation was also encouraging. Different races and religions learned to live together. Many governments cared deeply about human rights. There were huge improvements in education. Writers and artists came up with brilliant new ideas. All sorts of exciting new forms of entertainment were available, too.

Whichever way you look at it, it was indeed an amazing century.

► All the way to the USA! The culture of Hollywood, represented by the smiling face of Mickey Mouse, became the culture of the whole world.

# EMPIRES AND NATIONS

In the 15th century Europeans started forcing their way of life on the rest of the world. Explorers and traders went first, followed by missionaries, soldiers and governors. Helped by their advanced technology, particularly in weapons, they seized many lands around the globe. These lands were known as colonies.

The colonies were gathered together in empires. Thousands of Europeans went abroad to live in the colonies. In due course most of the colonies in the Americas rebelled against their European masters and became independent nations. But in the later 19th century there was a fresh wave of empire building ("imperialism"). By 1900 the European empires were bigger than ever.

## THE POWER OF EUROPE

The British Empire, headed by Queen Victoria, was the largest the world had ever seen. It included Australia and Canada and dozens of islands in every ocean, from tropical Trinidad to the icy Falklands. The British also ruled India, the "jewel in the crown" of their empire, and had many colonies in Africa.

European nations had divided Africa between them in the second half of the 19th century. Apart from Britain, other areas went to France, Belgium, Germany, Portugal, and Italy. The French, Dutch, and Germans also had colonies in Southeast Asia. Even the United States, which had fought to leave the British Empire, seized islands in the Pacific and Caribbean.

Empires often brought great wealth to the "mother countries" that ruled them. Colonies supplied cheap materials, such as cotton, and bought Western-made goods in return. Empires also made their rulers feel superior to those they governed. This gave Westerners a false sense of their own importance. Some imperialists believed it was the "white man's burden" to spread their way of life around the world.

◀ Mahatma Gandhi (1869–1948), the father of non-violent protest. His campaign weakened British authority in India and led to the country's independence in 1947.

▶ Nelson Mandela, the first president of post-apartheid South Africa, hands the Rugby World Cup to his country's captain in 1995.

## SIGNS OF WEAKNESS

World War I (1914–18) shattered the countries of Europe. After four years of fighting, Germany was defeated. The victorious nations took over the colonies of those they had defeated. But the victors were tired and short of money, and they found their empires more of a problem than a help. Several countries where many Europeans had gone to live, such as Canada, Australia, and New Zealand, were already governing themselves.

Ideas were also changing. Instead of being proud of their empires, Europeans began to feel guilty about them. They realized that everyone, whatever their race or religion, had a right to govern themselves. The people of the colonies were eager for independence, too. Some followed the example of India's Mahatma Gandhi and opposed European rule peacefully. Others, such as the Sanusi of Libya, used violence.

▶ A proud painting of German troops with the six-nation force that put down China's "Boxer" rebellion of 1900. The Boxers feared the colonial powers would slice up China "like a melon" and share it between them.

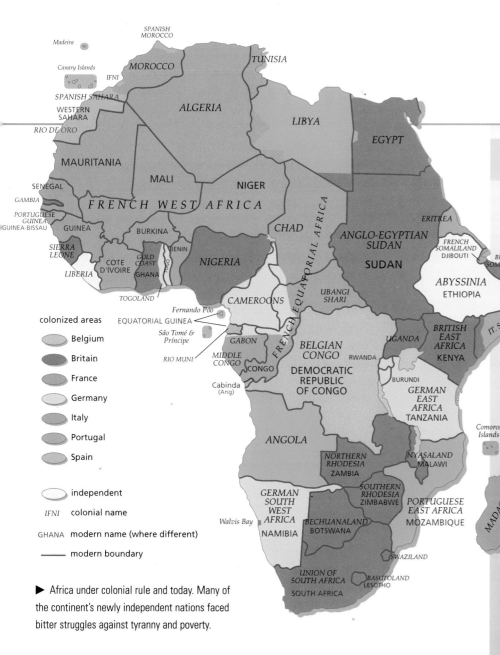

## colonized areas

- Belgium
- Britain
- France
- Germany
- Italy
- Portugal
- Spain

- independent
- *IFNI* colonial name
- GHANA modern name (where different)
- —— modern boundary

▶ Africa under colonial rule and today. Many of the continent's newly independent nations faced bitter struggles against tyranny and poverty.

## THE EMPIRES COLLAPSE

World War II (1939–45) left the colonial powers so weak that they could no longer hold their empires together. India was the first large colony to become an independent country after World War II. When the British handed over power in 1947, they divided the country between India and the Muslim state of Pakistan. Several other Asian countries, from Syria to Indonesia, also became independent in the 1940s.

Once the breakup of the empires had started, it was impossible to stop. The Vietnamese drove out the French in 1954. By the end of the 1950s the African states of Egypt, Sudan, Guinea, and Ghana all governed themselves. They were joined during the 1960s by the rest of Africa and most of the Caribbean.

## ▶ EMPIRES AND NATIONS

**1901** The Australian colonies join in a single, self-governing country.

**1902** Britain defeats the Boers (Dutch settlers) in South Africa and takes over the country.

**1917** Russian Revolution brings down the Russian empire.

**1919–20** Treaties divide up the German, Austro-Hungarian, and Turkish Empires and set up Yugoslavia and Czechoslovakia.

**1923** Egypt becomes an independent nation.

**1931** Commonwealth of Nations is set up as a free association of countries that had once been British colonies.

**1946** Syria and Jordan become independent.

**1947** India, Pakistan, and Ceylon (Sri Lanka) become independent.

**1948** Britain leaves Palestine, where the state of Israel is established.

**1949** Indonesia becomes independent.

**1952** Kenyan Mau Mau fight for independence.

**1954** French leave Vietnam and Cambodia.

**1956** Civil war breaks out in Algeria, which becomes independent in 1962.

**1957** Ghana becomes independent. Within 12 years all British and Belgian colonies in Africa are independent.

**1962–67** Most British colonies in the Caribbean become independent.

**1963** Malaysia becomes independent.

**1967–70** Civil war in Nigeria.

**1974–75** Portuguese colonies in Africa become independent.

**1991–95** Yugoslavia breaks up in bloody civil war.

**1994–96** Civil war in Rwanda.

**1994** White regime hands over power in South Africa.

**1997** Britain gives back the colony of Hong Kong to China.

## A WORLD OF NATIONS

The change from colony to independent country was not always easy. There was much unhappiness and fighting in India. Algeria fought long and hard to win freedom from France. For a long time the white people of Zimbabwe and South Africa refused to share power with people of other races.

Some new countries took time to settle down. Africa, in particular, was hit by poverty and violence. A bloody civil war rocked Nigeria (1967–70), and Uganda suffered under the cruel president Idi Amin (1971–80). Nevertheless, by the last quarter of the 20th century the European empires were gone for good, leaving the patchwork of independent nations we see today.

# FLYING AND DRIVING

Two inventions, the automobile and the airplane, rocked the modern world. They changed almost every part of people's lives, from work and leisure to the environment and even the way that wars were fought.

Karl Benz sold the first "motor wagons" in 1885. Early cars were expensive and often broke down. The first really popular car was Henry Ford's Model T (1908). By 1921 his company was making a million cars a year, both in the United States and abroad. Seventy-five years later there were more than 100 million cars in the United States alone.

▶ Going nowhere fast! Traffic jams wasted time and caused dangerous pollution. By the 1990s most cities were trying to get people to use cars less, and public transportation more.

▶ The American businessman Henry Ford, inventor of the mass-produced motor car, with his first motor buggy and his 10 millionth Model T. By 1920 half the world's cars were Model Ts.

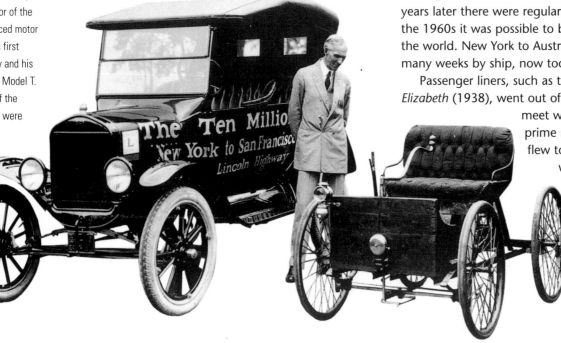

## WORLD ON WHEELS

Automobiles gave people enormous freedom to travel where they wanted, when they wanted. They could drive to work far from home or a railway station. In their leisure time they could visit distant friends and take interesting vacations. Shopping became easier at out-of-town malls. To meet motorists' needs, motels, drive-in restaurants, banks, and movie theaters were built.

Although the automobile industry made millions of new jobs, the use of the car brought problems. People lost the habit of bicycling or walking and became unfit. Railways shut down and many city centers were left bleak and empty. Pavement spread like molasses over the countryside. Accidents killed and maimed millions. Noise and exhaust fumes polluted the air. By the end of the century some said that, like Frankenstein, we had created a monster we could not control.

## TAKEOFF

The first planes, with spluttering engines and fragile frames, were little more than costly toys. Less than 20 years later there were regular passenger air services. By the 1960s it was possible to book a flight to anywhere in the world. New York to Australia, which in 1914 took many weeks by ship, now took less than a day by plane.

Passenger liners, such as the 80,000-ton *Queen Elizabeth* (1938), went out of business. Politicians could meet within hours, as when British prime minister Neville Chamberlain flew to Munich in 1938 to talk with Adolf Hitler. Letters whizzed around the world, and each day aircraft carried sports teams, business people, and tourists to places their grandparents had hardly heard of.

▲ The remarkable BAC Harrier could take off and land vertically. Many of the major advances in aircraft technology first appeared in military planes.

## BEYOND THE SKIES

The jet engine was invented just before World War II and was soon used to drive aircraft. Rocket power followed shortly afterwards. By 1961 the Russians had a man in space. Eight years later the Americans were on the Moon. Every year brought fresh discoveries and new challenges as the masters of Earth began exploring space, the final frontier.

► An astronaut floats in space high above Earth. Space travel was science fiction come true, but it was too expensive for mass transport. A spacesuit alone cost $10 million.

## ▶ FLYING AND DRIVING

**1900** German Graf von Zeppelin makes first gas-filled airship.

First Mercedes car is built by Gottlieb Daimler for Emile Jellinek, who names it after his daughter Mercedes.

**1903** *Flyer* makes the first steady flight by a heavier-than-air machine. Built by engineers Orville and Wilbur Wright, the plane flies 260 meters on the beach at Kitty Hawk, North Carolina.

**1907** Frenchman Paul Cornu makes first helicopter flight.

**1909** Frenchman Louis Blériot flies across the English Channel.

**1912** "Unsinkable" liner *Titanic* hits an iceberg and sinks.

**1913** Ford begins building Model T cars on a moving assembly line.

**1914** Panama Canal opens.

**1919** Public air service between Berlin and Weimar, Germany.

Alcock and Brown cross the Atlantic in a Vickers Vimy plane.

**1925** One of first motels opens in California.

**1932** Cologne–Bonn motorway opens. By the end of the century highways crisscross the world.

**1936** Volkswagen ("people's car") begin making their famous "Beetle" car.

**1939** German Heinkel He-178 makes first jet flight.

**1944** Germans launch V2 rockets. The first long-range guided missiles prepare the way for space exploration.

**1951** Drive-in movie theaters opening all over the U.S.

**1955** U.S. begins its network of interstate highways.

**1957** Man-made satellite launched. Russia's 183.7 lb. *Sputnik I* circles the Earth every 95 minutes.

**1959** Mini car manufactured.

SRN-1 Hovercraft flies across the English Channel.

**1961** Yuri Gagarin the first person in space.

**1963** Russian Valentina Tereshkova the first woman in space.

**1969** Neil Armstrong sets foot on the moon. Watched by millions of TV viewers, the astronaut says it is, "One small step for a man, one giant leap for mankind."

**1970** Boeing 747 "Jumbo" jet enters service. It carries twice as many passengers as any other plane.

**1971** Russians launch *Salyut 1* space station.

**1978** U.S. *Pioneer* spacecraft reaches Venus.

**1981** Reusable space shuttle *Columbia* makes first flight.

**1994** Channel Tunnel between Britain and France opened.

**1997** U.S. *Pathfinder* spacecraft makes soft landing on Mars.

*Thrust SSC* jet-powered car becomes first land vehicle to go supersonic.

# THE RIGHTS OF WOMEN

During the 19th century a few women began demanding the right to vote. Their campaign continued, with much success, into the 20th century. After World War II women started asking for an equal chance with men in jobs, education, and pay. In many countries they got what they wanted; in others their requests were turned down. Some women, including many Muslims, did not want the same rights and duties as men. Even so, the question of women's rights could not be ignored.

## SECOND-CLASS HUMAN BEINGS

When the century began, women were generally thought less able than men. In only one country—New Zealand—could they vote in elections. Compared with men, they were poorly educated and paid. It was very rare to find a woman doctor, lawyer, or politician. There were no women priests.

Women were taught to see themselves as second-class human beings. They were often ill-treated, too. In some old-fashioned parts of the world they were not allowed to choose their husbands. After marriage their husbands "owned" them and could do most anything they wanted with them. In China, where small feet were admired, girls' feet were tightly bound to stop them from growing, and fathers sometimes killed unwanted girl babies.

Attitudes and customs like these had existed for centuries. Religion and tradition kept them in place. People who wanted to change things were labeled as rebels.

▼ If men can vote, why can't we? A bus load of British "suffragettes" campaigning for the right to vote, 1905. When their request was turned down, they used more violent tactics, such as setting fire to the contents of mailboxes.

◄ Small is beautiful —in men's eyes. A Chinese woman displays a foot deformed by binding since childhood.

## NEW SOCIETIES, NEW WOMEN

The major religions were run by men. In places where religion became less important (like western Europe), women gradually got a more equal say in what went on. Women did well in industrial countries because they could handle machines and keep accounts just as well as men.

The spread of democracy helped women, too. When all men were allowed to vote, it was difficult to see why all women could not do so too. The spread of birth control also helped women. In 1900 married women spent much of their time having children and caring for them. A family of twelve or more was quite common. Wives had little time for life outside the home. But once they learned how to limit the size of their families, they were free to get a better education and take interesting jobs.

Women themselves led the movement for new thinking. The most important were hard-hitting campaigners (like Susan B. Anthony and Australia's Germaine Greer) and successful politicians (like Sri Lanka's prime minister Sirimavo Bandaranaike and Argentina's Eva Peron).

▶ A 1960s Chinese poster urging men and women to respect each other and work together, even on a building site.

六、关心同志，尊师爱徒，和睦家庭，团结邻里。

## VOTES ARE NOT ENOUGH

During the first part of the century women wanted to be equal with men in politics. Finland was the first European country to allow women to vote, China the first Asian country. The arrival of communism, which accepted equality between the sexes, helped the women's cause. So too did world war. When most young men were away fighting, women successfully took over "men's work," such as farming and bus driving.

Even so, many women still believed it was a man's world. Husbands expected their wives to look after the house and children like unpaid servants, and women found it difficult to get to the top in business, professional jobs, and politics. So in the 1960s a second campaign began, called "feminism." It taught women to be proud of themselves and be equal with men in everything. Some countries passed laws making it illegal for jobs to be given to men rather than equally qualified women.

The new ideas produced great changes in societies that accepted them. More women chose to follow careers rather than have children. Some rose to important positions in business. Indira Gandhi and Margaret Thatcher were among the most powerful leaders of their day. Women even served as front-line soldiers.

Not everyone welcomed these changes. Feminism made little progress in the poorer countries. Some Muslims and Roman Catholics told women to behave as they had always done and stick to being wives and mothers. The world was happier, they taught, when the two sexes followed their own separate, traditional paths.

## ▶ THE RIGHTS OF WOMEN

**1900** Sex education begins in German schools.

Women take part in Olympic Games.

**1902** Foot-binding banned in China.

**1903** Emmeline Pankhurst sets up Women's Social and Political Union to campaign for votes for women in Britain.

**1904** Woman arrested for smoking on a New York street.

**1906** Finland gives women the right to vote. The next year the Finns elect women to parliament.

**1913** Emily Davison killed when she throws herself under the king's horse in the Derby. She is protesting women not being allowed to vote.

**1916** First birth control clinic opens in U.S.

**1917** Russia sets up first women's army unit.

Women given the right to vote in the USSR.

**1920** U.S. constitution changed to give women the right to vote.

**1925** Chinese women given the right to vote.

**1926** Indian women allowed to be elected to government.

**1934** Women tennis players allowed to wear shorts at Wimbledon.

Turkish women allowed to vote.

**1944** British women teachers allowed to marry.

**1949** Simone de Beauvoir's book *The Second Sex* is published. She argues that men and women are born similar but are made different by their upbringing.

**1960** Sirimavo Bandaranaike first elected woman leader, Sri Lanka.

**1961** Women Strike for Peace movement set up in U.S. It campaigns against the Cold War and the Vietnam War.

**1963** Betty Friedan's book *The Feminine Mystique* attacks the idea that women can be only wives and mothers. Feminist movement begins.

**1975** Junko Tabei is first woman to climb Mount Everest.

**1979** Margaret Thatcher prime minister of Britain.

**1980** Iranian women protest about strict dress laws.

**1985** Nairobi conference ends United Nations Decade for Women.

**1989** Barbara Harris becomes an Episcopal bishop in the U.S.

**1995** UN Conference on Women held in Beijing, China.

◀ Many Muslim women insisted that true freedom meant sticking to traditional ways, such as wearing the veil in public.

# ARMED CONFLICT

A different kind of war scarred the 20th century. New types of weapon—the machine gun, airplane, submarine, and tank—became just as important as human bravery. Several wars were "total": no one was safe from the bomb or missile, and nations had to direct all their efforts into the war. Finally, newspapers, radio, film, and, later, TV made every action instant news.

## THE TECHNOLOGY OF WAR

By 1915 machine guns controlled land war. On the Western Front during World War I, a few machine guns often stopped the advance of thousands of soldiers. Tanks speeded war up again. They made it possible for the Nazi armies to sweep quickly across Europe at the beginning of World War II. By the 1970s, anti-tank guns and mines were again making swift advance difficult.

In 1900 battleships were the most powerful weapon afloat. By the World War II battles of Coral Sea and Midway, when the two sides were out of each other's sight, the battleship era was over. Now aircraft carriers and submarines held the key to naval success.

Airplanes changed war completely. The early ones dropped explosive or gas bombs far behind the front line. In 1945 the United States used the first nuclear bombs. Then came missiles, some carrying horrible chemical and biological warheads.

▼ The nightmare of technological warfare. Russian officers in gas masks during World War I. Because they were afraid of retaliation, neither side used gas in World War II.

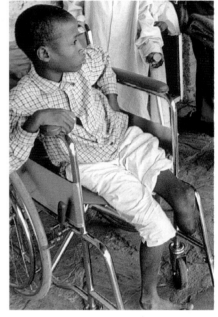

▶ A Tutsi boy with an amputated leg (1994), one of the many millions of innocent civilian victims of 20th-century warfare.

## WORLD WAR

Many thought the European war of August 1914 would be over by Christmas. In fact, the "Great War" lasted for over four years and spread to become a world war. Fighting took place in the Far East, Africa, the Middle East, and at sea. It was heaviest in Europe, where the Allied Powers (France, Britain, Italy, Russia, and their allies) eventually defeated the Central Powers (Germany, Austria-Hungary, Turkey, and their allies). Over 9 million soldiers were killed. They became known as Europe's "Lost Generation."

World War II was on an even larger scale. It began in China, flared up in Europe, and spread to the United States in 1941.

Airplanes and conquering armies brought the war to millions of ordinary people. By 1945 the conflict affected virtually everyone in the world in one way or another.

The destruction was terrible. Some 100,000 people died during a two-day bombing raid on Dresden (February 13–14, 1945). Perhaps a million died during the 900-day siege of Leningrad (1941–44), and on August 6, 1945, a single atomic bomb wiped out the Japanese city of Hiroshima.

##  ARMED CONFLICT

**1899–1902** Anglo-Boer War in South Africa.

**1904–5** Russo-Japanese War.

**1914–18** World War I.

**1916** Battle of Verdun. The German failure to break the French line leaves both armies exhausted.

**1918** German Spring Offensive. Germany's attempt to win the war on the Western Front before U.S. might comes into play ends in failure.

**1918–21** Russian Civil War.

**1936–9** Spanish Civil War.

**1937** Japan and China go to war. The conflict marks the beginning of World War II in the Far East.

**1939** War breaks out in Europe when Hitler invades Poland.

**1941** USSR and U.S. enter World War II. All the world's major powers now at war.

**1944** Allies land in France.

**1945** Atomic bomb dropped on Hiroshima.

**1946–9** Chinese Civil War. The conflict continues fighting that began in the 1920s.

**1948–9** First Arab–Israeli War. The bitter conflict flares up again in 1967 and 1973.

**1950–3** Korean War. The U.S. and other democratic nations fight to contain communism in Southeast Asia.

**1964–75** Vietnam War.

**1979** Soviet troops invade Afghanistan.

**1980–8** Iran–Iraq War.

**1990** Iraq invades Kuwait. In 1991 United Nations troops, including U.S. high-tech armed forces, defeat the Iraqis.

**1992–5** Bosnian Civil War.

▼ Nuclear weapons—the end of the world or the end of world war? Fear of a nuclear holocaust may have prevented the USSR and the United States from going to war, 1947–89.

◀▲ The changing face of warfare. Paintings of a cavalry action in the Russo-Japanese War (1904–5) and Kamikaze suicide bombers attacking a battleship in 1945.

## FLASHPOINTS

Many smaller wars were waged over territory. Before World War I, Britain fought the Boers (Dutch settlers) to control South Africa, and Russia fought Japan to control parts of eastern Asia. In the 1930s Italy used a squabble over land as an excuse to attack Abyssinia (Ethiopia). Iran and Iraq fought a long and cruel war (1980–88), using chemical and biological weapons, over territory on the Persian Gulf.

People also went to war because of their different ideas. Communists and their enemies plunged Russia and China into bloody civil wars. In the 1930s Spain was torn by an equally terrible civil war. In the second half of the century the United States fought major wars against the communists in Korea and Vietnam.

Some colonies, like Algeria, fought for their freedom. Independence did not necessarily bring peace, however. When governments could not keep control, civil wars broke out in newly independent nations, such as Congo (Zaire) and Nigeria. War also followed the collapse of communism in Europe. The worst affected area was the Balkans, where World War I had begun 80 years before.

## TERRORISM, THE UNOFFICIAL WAR

Terrorists fought several long, drawn out, and heartbreaking struggles. World War I started when a terrorist shot Archduke Franz Ferdinand of Austria in Sarajevo. European powers often faced terrorism in Africa, the Middle East, and Asia. The British, for example, fought against terrorist freedom fighters in Kenya (the Mau-Mau), Palestine, and Iraq.

Minority groups, such as the Spanish Basques and the republicans of Northern Ireland (the IRA), used terrorism to draw attention to their cause. The Arabs who attacked Israel from neighboring countries were always in the news. The Black September terrorists made the headlines everywhere when, in September 1972, they raided the Munich Olympics. Nine Israeli athletes and five Arabs died.

# IMAGES AND WORDS

Twentieth-century art was full of change and experiment. It used new materials and broke old rules to capture the hectic and unsure mood of the times. Painters discovered fresh ways of looking at the world. Musicians explored unusual rhythms and sounds. Writers examined areas of life that previous generations had turned away from. Light-hearted art merged with the serious, and a new world culture developed.

## BREAKING THE RULES

Up-to-date painters and sculptors were not interested in being "realistic." They used shape and color to capture the spirit of their subject, rather than how it might look. Portraits by the famous Spanish artist Pablo Picasso, for example, showed the side and front of a person's face at the same time. The sculptor Henry Moore simplified human bodies into huge, rounded figures with holes in them. Abstract artists produced pictures that did not look *like* anything—Jackson Pollock, for instance, produced pictures by dripping and splattering paint onto the canvas. Later, artists used everyday objects, even building bricks, in their work.

▼ The Spanish artist Pablo Picasso (1881–1973) with two of his best-known works. Not everyone liked his paintings, but no one could ignore their power and originality

▲ "Pop" artists such as Andy Warhol turned images from comic books, soup cans, and other everyday objects into works of art.

Musicians broke new ground, too. The Russian composer Igor Stravinsky was one of many who experimented with new rhythms and sounds. Others mixed the music and instruments of different countries. There was electronic music, too, and music without melody or obvious rhythm. In a piece called *4 minutes 33 seconds*, the pianist sat at the piano and didn't play a note, leaving the audience to listen to the sounds around them that they would never normally notice.

Writers also broke the rules, exploring new ways of writing books, plays, and poetry. e e cummings wrote poems without punctuation or capital letters. James Joyce wrote his novel *Ulysses* (1922) as the thoughts of the characters— a mix of ideas, facts, and dreams. Other writers told stories backwards, or wove together several tales and left the reader to untangle them.

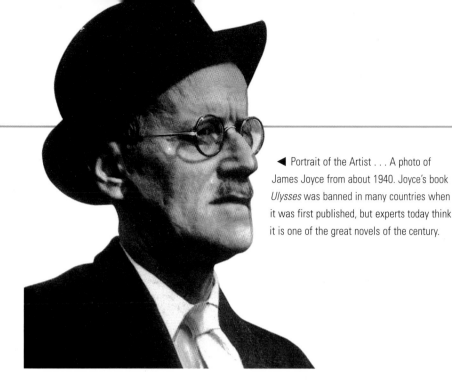

◄ Portrait of the Artist . . . A photo of James Joyce from about 1940. Joyce's book *Ulysses* was banned in many countries when it was first published, but experts today think it is one of the great novels of the century.

## NEVER THE SAME AGAIN

Years of rule-breaking and experimentation brought astonishing changes in the arts. But not everyone liked what had happened. They complained that the arts had become too complicated. Ordinary people, they said, wanted pictures they could recognize, tuneful music, and books that were easy to read.

Even so, the rule-breakers left their mark. Their ideas spread beyond the world of art and into many areas of everyday life, from wallpaper design to rock music and TV drama. They also helped bring together different traditions to produce a new international culture. Among the most exciting developments was the way Asian, South American, and African writers brought fresh energy and richness to the Western idea of novel-writing.

## STEEL, GLASS, AND PLASTIC

Much of 20th-century architecture was confident and forward-looking. Its most original new buildings were multi-story towers of concrete, steel, and glass. Skyscrapers were the temples of the new age, built to the glory of business and wealth. The most famous skyscraper skyline grew up during the 1920s in Manhattan, New York City. Sixty years later skyscrapers loomed over almost every major city in the world.

Steel, concrete, and glass were also used for a range of other buildings. Some, such as the Sydney Opera House, were brilliantly original. The same could not be said of the ugly apartment blocks that sprouted in suburbs the world over. Although they were more comfortable than the slums and hovels in which many families still lived, they were often bleak and lonely.

Designers, like architects, welcomed new materials. Starting in the 1920s, brightness and light were all the rage. Artificial dyes and fabrics brought exciting new ranges of color and texture. Kitchens were transformed from sooty places of wood and iron to rooms gleaming with stainless steel, plastic, and enamel. The changes in car design were fascinating. Early cars simply looked like carriages without horses. By the 1950s they were like silvery spaceships. Forty years later they had become brightly colored bubbles.

▼ The soaring sails of the Sydney Opera House in Australia (built 1959–73) captured the hopeful spirit of a young country.

## ▶ IMAGES AND WORDS

**1900** Sigmund Freud's book *The Interpretation of Dreams* published. Freud's ideas about the mind's subconscious thoughts had an enormous influence on writers, artists, and thinkers.

**1908** Georges Braque's cube-like landscape *Trees at L'Estaque* signals the start of the Cubism movement in painting.

**1913** Igor Stravinsky's ballet music *The Rite of Spring* first performed in Paris. It lays the foundation for much modern music.

**1919** Bauhaus design school opens in Germany. Its work links design with modern technology.

**1922** T. S. Eliot's *The Waste Land* offers a gloomy view of life after World War I.

**1924** George Gershwin's *Rhapsody in Blue* combines classical music and jazz.

**1931** Empire State Building completed.

**1936** Penguin begins to publish paperback books.

**1937** Picasso's anti-war painting *Guernica*.

**1945** George Orwell's satire *Animal Farm* published.

**1946** Jackson Pollock starts his drip paintings.

**1949** Mies van der Rohe designs Promontory Apartments, a glass and steel skyscraper in Chicago. Similar buildings soon appear all over the world.

**1952** First performance of John Cage's piece *4 minutes, 33 seconds*.

Architect Le Corbusier finishes his Unité d'Habitation apartment block in Marseille.

**1959** Guggenheim Museum of Art opens in New York. It was designed by U.S. architect Frank Lloyd Wright.

**1961** Andy Warhol pioneers "pop art."

**1967** Publication of Gabriel García Márquez's magical-realist novel *One Hundred Years of Solitude*.

**1977** Opening of the Pompidou Center in Paris, designed by British architect Richard Rogers. It was one of the first "see-through" buildings.

**1982** Alice Walker's novel about racist and sexual oppression, *The Color Purple*, becomes an international best-seller.

**1988** Salman Rushdie forced to go into hiding when Iran's strict Muslim regime condemns his novel *The Satanic Verses*.

**1991** Controversial artist Damien Hirst exhibits the preserved body of a 4-meter shark in a tank.

# BODY AND MIND

In 1911 the Irish playwright George Bernard Shaw said doctors were no more reliable than fortune tellers. By the end of the century, when many killer diseases could be prevented or cured and amazing operations performed, Shaw's advice looked foolish. In 1900 good health was a blessing. In the 1990s millions took it for granted. Doctors had become the priests of a new god—medicine.

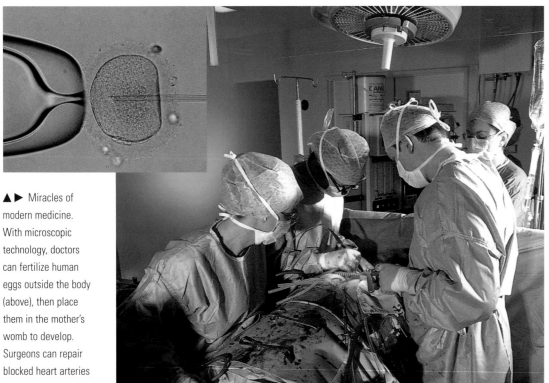

▲▶ Miracles of modern medicine. With microscopic technology, doctors can fertilize human eggs outside the body (above), then place them in the mother's womb to develop. Surgeons can repair blocked heart arteries by replacing them with veins taken from the patient's leg (right).

## TAKE THIS MEDICINE

Chemists and doctors produced a medical revolution. Aspirin, the first wonder drug, appeared early in the century. It was followed by a stream of amazing pills and medicines. Perhaps the two most important were the birth-control pill, which went on sale in the 1960s, and antibiotics. Other medicines treated diabetes, lowered blood pressure, lifted depression, and fought cancers and many other illnesses.

Doctors also used new vaccinations and inoculations to prevent disease. Babies in wealthier nations were injected to protect them from all kinds of illnesses that had once been fatal. A vaccine against polio was widely available by the 1950s. One of the greatest triumphs was wiping out the disease smallpox.

## SURGERY

In 1900 surgery—cutting into the body—was a long and risky business. Taking out an appendix, for example, was a major operation. Patients could be made unconscious and infection could be controlled, but even so, many died. Treatment was also very expensive—only the wealthy could afford it.

New drugs and ways of making people unconscious gradually made surgery much safer. Doctors learned a lot from helping the wounded during World War I. From the 1940s onwards new drugs (antibiotics) were developed that could kill the bacteria that caused disease and infection. This allowed doctors to carry out more complicated operations. As early as 1914 surgeons operated on a dog's heart, and by the 1960s human heart surgery was quite common. By 1961 surgeons were fitting artificial hip joints. Six years later a South African surgeon transplanted a heart from one person to another. Laser surgery began in the 1980s. Within ten years surgeons could operate on almost every organ, from the brain to the big toe.

▶ The ravages of smallpox. Those who survived it were usually left with horrible scars. Wiping out the disease was one of the World Health Organization's greatest triumphs.

◄ The humiliation of mental illness. Patients being washed by staff in a mental institution in 1930.

## INSIDE THE MIND

Psychology (the scientific study of how we behave) began in the late 19th century. Thanks to the work of the Austrian doctor Sigmund Freud and his followers, by the early 20th century scientists were beginning to get a clearer picture of how the human mind worked. A new vocabulary appeared. It included phrases now used in everyday speech, such as "inferiority complex." When doctors started taking this work seriously, psychiatry—the treatment of mental illness—began.

Progress was slow. Troops who broke down under fire during World War I were labeled as "cowards" by doctors. Many years later, people suffering from mental illness were still being called "mad." But at least a start had been made towards understanding this most interesting and complicated branch of medicine.

## NEW FRONTIERS, NEW PROBLEMS

As some problems were solved, fresh ones appeared. New types of viruses and bacteria grew up that resisted drugs. The typical 20th-century Western lifestyle—high stress, unhealthy diet, and little exercise—led to more cancers and heart disease. In some areas, such as Scotland, heart disease spread like an epidemic.

By the middle of the century richer countries were trying to provide medical care for all citizens. But new treatments and drugs were very expensive. As a result, by the 1990s doctors were concentrating on preventing disease, not just curing it. Better medicine meant that people lived longer, and was one reason why the world's population grew so fast. Governments had to spend more on pensions and care for the elderly.

Medical science raised alarming moral questions, too. Advances in genetics made it possible for scientists to grow spare parts from human tissues and to produce human embryos outside the body. These medical advances were welcome, but they raised fears that it would soon be possible to make clones (exact copies) of complete human beings. The idea of cloning human beings was completely unacceptable to many people.

## ▶ BODY AND MIND

**1900** Sigmund Freud, pioneer of modern psychology, publishes *The Interpretation of Dreams*.

**1912** Word "vitamin" coined for substances needed in very small quantities in diet. Many vitamin-deficiency diseases are soon being cured.

**1922** Insulin injections first given to diabetes sufferers.

**1928** Penicillin, the first antibiotic, discovered. The drug does not come into general use for another 15 years.

**1944** Kidney machine first used to treat kidney failure.

**1952** First successful sex-change operation.

**1953** James Watson and Francis Crick discover DNA, the basic genetic material.

**1954** American doctors suggest link between smoking and cancer. Their findings are confirmed in 1964.

Polio vaccine available for general use.

**1961** The birth-control pill goes on sale in the U.S.

First hip replacements made.

**1967** First heart transplant made. The patient survives for 18 days.

**1968** Vaccine for meningitis available.

**1969** First fertilization of a human egg outside the body.

**1975** Body scanner invented.

**1980** Smallpox eradicated from Earth.

**1981** AIDS recognized in the U.S.

**1984** Scientists able to identify individual DNA (genetic fingerprinting).

Baboon's heart transplanted into a girl. She survives for 20 days.

**1985** Laser surgery developed.

**1997** Dolly the sheep artificially produced by cloning.

◄ Prevention is better than cure. By the last quarter of the century doctors were advising everyone to exercise regularly as a way of fighting off disease.

**17**

# GETTING AND SPENDING

Over the century the world's population rose from 1.65 billion to more than 6 billion. Cities and towns expanded alarmingly. In 1900 only about 10 percent of people lived in cities. By 2000 this had risen to over 55 percent. São Paulo in Brazil had 40,000 inhabitants in 1900, 2.5 million in 1950, and a staggering 17 million by 1990.

More people meant more food, houses, clothes, and goods like pots and pans. The better-off also wanted more consumer goods, such as cars, fridges, and computers. The opportunities for those who made these things were enormous.

## BOOMING BUSINESS

At the beginning of the century the United States overtook Britain and Germany as the leading business and industrial country. United States dollars soon replaced British pounds as the world's most important money. Two of the biggest industries, automobiles and computers, started in the United States. American business was so successful that other countries studied and copied its methods.

In the first half of the century most of the world's factories were in the U.S. or Europe. Western countries controlled world trade, too. After 1945, industry began to spread more widely around the world. By the 1980s goods made in countries like Japan, India, or China were just as good as (and often cheaper than) those made in the West. Japan did particularly well after World War II and became one of the world's richest countries.

Huge new companies grew up. Toyota and ICI, for example, traded in dozens of countries. Firms paid a lot of attention to their image, with stylish logos and expensive advertising campaigns. Groups of nations, such as the European Union, realized they did better if they cooperated. By the 1990s most industrial countries were much, much richer than they had been a century earlier.

◀ Eastern promise. By the mid-1990s the British colony of Hong Kong (now returned to China) had become one of the world's richest cities.

▼ New wealth, old customs. Although oil wealth made the Arabs of the Persian Gulf among the richest people in the world, they did not lose touch with their traditional way of life.

▶ Playing with money, 1923. German children use banknotes as building blocks because inflation (the falling value of money) had made them worthless. In October 1923 $1.00 was worth almost 1.5 billion German marks.

## ▶ GETTING AND SPENDING

**1901** Oil discovered in Texas.

Instant coffee invented.

**1913** Model T Fords built on a moving assembly line.

**1923** A supermarket opens in San Francisco.

**1929** Wall Street crash begins the Great Depression. The value of many companies collapses, ruining millions of Americans. The Depression soon spreads to all capitalist countries.

**1933** U.S. president Roosevelt announces his New Deal package to deal with the Depression. By now 33% of all German workers and 25% of all U.S. workers are without work.

**1945** International Monetary Fund and World Bank established.

**1946** Electronic computer built in U.S.

**1946–47** British government takes over (nationalizes) the coal, electricity, and railway industries

**1948** McDonald brothers open their first drive-in hamburger café.

**1954** Transistor radios on sale; shopping mall opens in Northland, Michigan.

**1957** European Community (now European Union) set up.

**1969** Japan's economy overtakes West Germany's.

**1971** Intel produces the microprocessor.

**1973** Cut in Arab oil production causes world-wide economic problems.

**1980s** Many governments sell off ("privatize") state-owned businesses.

**1982** CDs on sale.

**1987** World population reaches 5 billion.

**1989** Communist economic system collapses in Eastern Europe.

**1997–8** Serious depression in the fast-growing "tiger" countries of Southeast Asia.

◀ Poverty amid plenty—New York, 1979. At the end of the century most wealthy countries still had an "underclass" of poor people who missed out on the prosperity enjoyed by everyone else.

## BOOM AND DEPRESSION

Things did not get steadily better. Even the wealthy countries went through hard times (depressions), when there were not enough jobs or when prices rose rapidly. The Great Depression of the 1930s was particularly difficult. It made almost everyone worse off. Lots of people suffered during wartime, too.

After World War II, the prosperous countries set up organizations like the International Monetary Fund to stop another serious depression from happening. There were still difficulties, however, as when the price of oil rose sharply in the mid-1970s. Nevertheless, in the second half of the century wealth grew faster than ever before. Average Americans, were for example, twice as well off in 1970 as they had been in 1945.

▶ The wall comes down, 1989. The citizens of East (communist) and West (capitalist) Berlin celebrate the pulling down of the wall that had divided their city since 1961.

## THE RISE AND FALL OF COMMUNISM

In Western countries people were free to make and sell what they wanted. This was known as the capitalist system. In 1917 Russia tried another system, known as communism. Russia's communist government controlled jobs, industries, and prices. After World War II China and the countries of eastern Europe also became communist.

During the Great Depression it looked as if capitalism did not work. Some governments began to mix capitalist and communist ideas. The British government, for example, took over the railways and coal mines for the people. In the long run, however, capitalism came out on top. Russia did not do as well as its Western neighbors and in the 1990s it gave up communism. By then China, too, was beginning to water down its communism.

# BIG BROTHER IS WATCHING

In 1949 the British writer George Orwell wrote a book called *1984*. It was a horrible prediction about what might happen if we let governments get too powerful. No one was free in *1984*. The government forced people to use a new language—"Newspeak"—and even controlled their thoughts. Wherever people went, they were warned, "Big Brother is watching you." Big Brother was a dictator. Orwell got his ideas from what had happened during the first half of the century.

## COMMUNISM

The theory of communism was fine—all people should be treated equally and all goods and property should be shared. The problem was how to carry out these ideas. Until everyone was ready for the new ways, a handful of avid communists would run the country for the good of the people. This allowed dictators to seize power and rule for their own benefit. Another difficulty was that people who worked hard did not like earning the same as shirkers.

Russia was the first country to become communist. Lenin's communists seized power in 1917, removed everyone who opposed them, and controlled the country (which they called the Soviet Union or USSR) until 1991. Between 1928 and 1953 all power was in the hands of Stalin, a ruthless dictator. After World War II, the USSR forced Eastern Europe to accept communism, too.

In 1949 China came under the control of the communist dictator Mao Zedong. The government took over private land and businesses. The state owned everything—farms, railways, and shops. Because the government ran clothing factories, all Chinese people ended up wearing the same style of clothes!

▼ A parade of German Nazi (fascist) troops, 1937. The Nazis loved exhibitions of this sort because they encouraged order, discipline, and mindless patriotism.

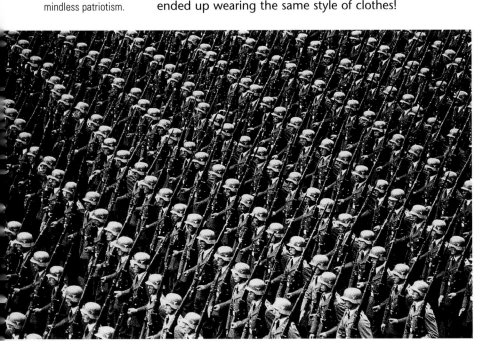

▲ Mao Zedong (central figure) urges all communists to work for a communist world—a Chinese poster of 1949.

## FASCISM

Fascism said it was the very opposite of communism. In fact, however, in many ways fascist countries were similar to communist ones. Strict and cruel dictators allowed their citizens little freedom. Italy became the first fascist country when Benito Mussolini came to power in 1922. Adolf Hitler, chosen to lead Germany in 1933, borrowed some of Mussolini's fascist ideas but carried them much further.

The key thing in a fascist country was service to the country and loyalty to its leader. All outsiders were enemies. The leader controlled or got rid of groups that got in his way, such as trade unions. The police could arrest anyone at any time on the flimsiest excuse. Prisoners had no chance of a fair trial.

## ▶ BIG BROTHER...

**1905** Communists fail to seize power in Russia.

**1917** Led by Vladimir Lenin, the communists take over Russia.

**1921** Chinese communist party established.

**1922** Mussolini, the first fascist dictator, comes to power in Italy.

**1925–26** Hitler sets out his ideas in *Mein Kampf* ("My Struggle").

**1928** Stalin becomes dictator of the USSR.

**1933** Hitler becomes chancellor of Germany. One of his first acts is to destroy the German communist party.

**1934** Hitler gets rid of Nazi opposition in the Night of the Long Knives.

**1936–38** Great Purge in the USSR.

**1937** Germany, Italy, and Japan form an anti-communist pact.

**1945** Fascist powers defeated in World War II.

**1946–91** Cold War between the West (led by the U.S.) and the East (led by the USSR). It is a period of hatred, mistrust, and misunderstanding but no actual fighting.

**1949** Mao Zedong's communists come to power in China.

**1953–64** Nikita Khrushchev runs the USSR. He criticizes some of the worst things Stalin had done.

**1959** Cuba becomes communist under Fidel Castro.

**1966** Mao Zedong begins a Cultural Revolution to keep himself in power. The revolution means violently challenging old-fashioned ways.

**1976** Death of Mao. China's new leaders start to relax the strictest aspects of Mao's communism.

**1985** Mikhail Gorbachev begins to reform Soviet communism. He calls his policies *glasnost* ("opening up") and *perestroika* ("re-organizing").

**1991** The USSR breaks up.

**1997** China allows Hong Kong to continue its non-communist ways.

## LIFE UNDER THE DICTATORS

Communist and fascist governments controlled the media. Newspapers, radio, and TV were allowed to tell the people only what the leader wanted them to hear. In Soviet Russia, for example, the radio news was full of the glorious things communists had done but hardly mentioned things that went wrong. Citizens who wanted to find out what was really happening tuned in to foreign stations like the BBC.

The dictators kept a firm grip on education. Their supporters rewrote history. Under communism this meant playing down the achievements of kings and praising the peasants and workers. In fascist Germany teachers taught their pupils to hate Jews. Children were encouraged to report suspicious teachers to the police.

The dictators governed by fear. The law was what they said it was, and nobody was safe. The police executed or sent to prison camps anyone who disagreed. In his Great Purge of 1936–38 Stalin had some 5 million people killed, including 90 percent of his army's generals, simply because he feared they might oppose him.

▲ Farewell communism! Lenin's statue is removed from Vilnius, Lithuania, in 1991.

▲ Idi "Dada" Amin, the kindly looking but cruel dictator who terrorized Uganda from 1971 to 1978.

## COLLAPSE AND CHANGE

Fascism ended with the defeat of Hitler and Mussolini in World War II. The USSR played a major part in this victory and in 1945 it seemed more powerful than ever. But its industry was backward and inefficient. As they saw their western neighbors getting freer and richer, the citizens of eastern Europe became fed up. They rebelled and replaced communism with capitalist democracy.

After Mao's death China also started to change. Its leaders realized that people liked to work for themselves, not the government. By the end of the century China was still communist, but its citizens enjoyed more freedom than in Mao's time.

◀ Members of a work brigade in a Russian labor camp in 1932, during the Stalinist period. Anyone who disagreed with Stalin's policies was arrested and forced to work under atrocious conditions.

# THAT'S SHOW BUSINESS!

"There's no business like show business," sang the chorus of *Annie Get Your Gun* in 1948. In 1900 people would have wondered what they were talking about. The most popular forms of entertainment were reading, family games, and local fairs or shows. Almost all music was played live. Only towns and cities had mass entertainment, such as theaters, music halls, and concerts.

All this changed over the course of the century. Entertainment became a multi-billion-dollar industry, selling the same TV programs, films, and songs all around the world. In the 1980s, North African nomads changed ancient travel habits to fit in with showings of the American soap opera *Dallas*!

## HOLLYWOOD

Four inventions sparked the entertainment revolution: movie film, recorded sound, radio, and TV. The cinema, just beginning in 1900, was most popular in the 1930s. Silent black-and-white films led to "talkies," then glitzy color movies. For a few cents audiences enjoyed glamour and excitement they never met in everyday life.

Different film styles developed. The French made detailed films about everyday life; the Indians went in for large-scale romantic ones. The most successful studios were in Hollywood, California. Its stars, such as Charlie Chaplin, Greta Garbo, Clint Eastwood, and Marilyn Monroe, were household names. So were Walt Disney's cartoon characters Mickey Mouse and Donald Duck.

▼ Dizzie Gillespie, the great American jazz composer, bandleader, and trumpeter. In the 1950s the U.S. government paid for his band's international tours.

▶ Hollywood was so excited by the performance of the glamorous Marlene Dietrich in Germany's first sound film, *The Blue Angel* (1930), they signed her up immediately and made her an international star.

## JAZZ TO RAP

Broadcasting, records, and tapes got the whole world singing. By the 1980s people could have music wherever they went, thanks to portable radios and stereos. Hit tunes were arranged in charts and Western dancing became freer and more exciting. Millions flocked to musical shows and pop concerts.

The biggest changes grew out of African-American music. Between the wars jazz and swing bands were in fashion. After World War II the strong, simple beat of rock 'n roll became popular around the world. In the 1960s and 1970s there was an explosion of rock and pop styles. In Jamaica, rock combined with Caribbean music to produce reggae, and later hip-hop and rap.

▲ The birth of a "world culture"—African children tuning in to Western TV programs beamed down by satellite.

## RADIO AND TV

Between 1920 and 1950, radio ruled home entertainment. It brought variety shows, music, drama, and news right into people's homes. An astonishing example of its influence was Orson Welles' drama *The War of the Worlds* (1938), about an invasion from Mars. It was so realistic many New Yorkers really believed Martians had landed!

Television grew rapidly from the mid-1950s. Sets became more reliable, color was introduced, and cable and satellite broadcasting increased the range of viewing. By the 1970s video recorders were turning millions of homes into mini-cinemas, and within a decade television-watching had become the world's favorite entertainment.

## BRIGHTER, BETTER, AND MORE

Because more people could read, the sale of books, newspapers, and magazines soared. The owners of newspapers—"press barons"—became very powerful. Cheap paperbacks appeared in the 1930s. To compete with TV, non-fiction books were made brighter and more lively. In the 1970s newspapers became more like magazines, using color and exciting design.

All kinds of new entertainment were dreamed up, from Monopoly to Frisbees. The invention of personal computers made games like Sonic the Hedgehog all the rage. Then came cyber pets, virtual reality, and still more ways of enjoying ourselves.

## ▶ THAT'S SHOW BUSINESS!

**1900** His Master's Voice (HMV) gramophone records go on sale.
R. A. Fessenden broadcasts speech by radio.

**1909** African American bandleader W. C. Handy writes "Memphis Blues."

**1911** Nestor Film Company opens a studio in Hollywood, California.

**1924** The Charleston dance craze.

**1925** Charlie Chaplin stars in *The Gold Rush* film.

**1926** Scotsman John Logie Baird transmits moving pictures.

**1927** *The Jazz Singer* "talkie" film.

**1928** First Mickey Mouse cartoon film.

**1929** Color pictures transmitted in U.S.

**1939** Hit film *Gone With the Wind* released.

**1943** Hit musical *Oklahoma!* opens in New York.

**1948** Long-playing (LP) records go on sale.

**1954** 19-year-old Elvis Presley makes his first record.

**1956** Video recorder developed. The first videos are the size of a small car.

**1960** The twist dance craze begins.

**1962** *Telstar* satellite sends live TV pictures across the Atlantic.

**1963** The Beatles release "Please Please Me." Within a year "Beatlemania" is sweeping the world.
Cassette tapes go on sale.

**1972** Computer games go on sale.

**1978** U.S. soap opera *Dallas* on TV.

**1981** Worldwide audience of 700 million watches wedding of Prince Charles and Lady Diana Spencer.

**1982** CDs go on sale.

**1992** CD-ROMs go on sale.

**1996** Computer-graphics film *Toy Story* released.

**1997** *Titanic*, the most expensive film ever made.

◀ Computer-generated heroes Woody the cowboy and spaceman Buzz Lightyear, starred in Walt Disney's *Toy Story*, the first computer-animated movie.

# RICH AND POOR

Human beings created more wealth in the 20th century than in all previous history. Tragically, it was not spread evenly around the world. The rich countries grew richer still. A handful of countries that had once been poor, like Saudi Arabia, came to share in these riches. But most poor countries remained so. In fact, by the end of the century the gap between the Haves and the Have-nots was wider than ever.

▲ 1992. The Haves... A chubby 10-year-old American enjoys a feast of junk food in front of his favorite TV program.

## THE RICH...

In 1900 most of the world's wealth lay in Europe and North America. Even here there were vast differences between the rich and poor. In Britain, for example, a mere 2 percent of the population owned three-quarters of the wealth.

Over the next 100 years (apart from the years of war and depression) the West got steadily more prosperous. By the 1980s several nations around the rim of the Pacific Ocean were also well off. In the richer countries welfare schemes, such as old-age pensions, helped tackle poverty. Nevertheless, homeless beggars still haunted the streets of cities such as New York and London in the 1990s.

Prosperity showed itself in all sorts of ways. Housing, diet, and education all improved. A throw-away society grew up. People rejected clothes and even cars when they became unfashionable, not when they wore out. Labor-saving devices, from vacuum cleaners to microwaves, filled their homes. Eating habits also changed. Pre-cooked, pre-packed food, eaten at all times of day and night, replaced the family meal prepared from raw ingredients. By the 1990s millions lived in material comfort that only kings had enjoyed in the past.

## ...AND THE POOR

War caused great poverty, especially among refugees. The Great Depression also led to widespread poverty, particularly in industrial countries. But the main reason why poverty increased was simply that there were many more people. The farmers in poor countries struggled to produce enough food in normal years. Bad harvests meant disaster. Some 5 million people died as a result of the Bengal famine in the early 1940s. By 1980 at least 500,000 million people lived close to starvation. The figure was rising each year.

As the West was building bathrooms and fitting electric lights, in the agricultural areas of Africa and Asia life went on as it had for centuries. People cooked their food over open fires, harvested crops by hand, and carried them to market in carts or baskets. Cars, running water, and electricity were the stuff of dreams. By the mid-1980s the United States had almost as many TV sets as viewers. In France the ratio was 1:2, in Malaysia 1:10, and in Uganda 1:200.

Unemployment remained a major cause of poverty. It was most obvious in the growing cities of the developing world, such as Calcutta in India. It was perhaps even more shocking in the West. Here, as wages rose, the gap between the employed and unemployed widened. This led to depression, vandalism, and crime.

◄ ...and the Have-nots. A destitute Somali mother gives her starving daughter a drink of water from a plastic jug.

▲ Poverty in London. A poor family in the East End, 1912. In his hand, the father holds a sheaf of pawn tickets.

## WHY?

The century's greatest scandal was that by the 1970s industry, commerce, and agriculture could have provided everyone on the planet with a reasonable standard of living. Why was this not done?

The main reason was the system known as capitalism. In countries that followed this system, businesses created wealth by competing with each other. The successful ones did well, the unsuccessful ones did not. To stand a chance in this system, the poorer countries needed educated workers and money for machinery. That meant borrowing, which in turn meant repaying debts with profits they made.

There were two ways around this problem. One was to swap capitalism for communism, which did not allow competition. This experiment failed because it took away people's freedom and made businesses inefficient.

The alternative was for developed countries to help their poorer neighbors by giving or lending them aid. Individuals, shocked by the reports of poverty, gave generously to organizations like Oxfam. Governments provided aid, too. Sweden gave 1% of its total annual wealth in development aid in 1980. Britain gave 0.5%, the United States, 0.2%.

Unfortunately, it was nowhere near enough.

◀ Rich and poor next door, Rio de Janeiro, Brazil. While the better-off lived in skyscraper apartments, their poor neighbors had to make do with shacks.

▶ A millionaire marriage in India. Although some Indians were among the poorest people on Earth, others (like these newlyweds) were among the richest.

# ▶ RICH AND POOR

**1901** More than 1 million die of famine in India.

**1906** British children given free school meals.

**1907** Washing machines on sale.

Famine threatens the lives of millions in China and Russia.

**1910** Food mixers on sale.

**1911** Russia exports almost 13 million tons of grain, even though 30 million Russians face starvation.

**1917** Clarence Birdseye freezes food to preserve it.

**1928** Starving Chinese are reported selling children to buy food.

**1932–34** 10–15 million Soviet citizens die of starvation.

**1937** U.S. introduces a limited minimum wage

**1942** Oxford Committee for Famine Relief (Oxfam) established.

The Beveridge Report calls for a "welfare state" in Britain to look after all citizens "from the cradle to the grave."

**1945** International Bank for Reconstruction and Development (World Bank) and International Monetary Fund established.

**1948** Microwave oven invented.

**1951** U.S. lends India $190 million to buy U.S. grain.

**1957** 20% of Americans said to be in poverty.

**1966** World food crisis. The U.S. had millions of tons of grain in storage, but the developing world could not afford to buy it

**1971** 77 developing countries demand a new world financial system.

**1980s** Droughts cause widespread famine in Africa.

Debts of some of the poorest countries cancelled.

**1980** The Brandt Report begs wealthy nations to show more concern for the developing world.

**1985** World agriculture producing more than 1,000 lbs. of cereals and root crops annually per head of population.

Live Aid rock concerts to raise money for famine relief in Ethiopia.

**1988** Rio de Janeiro Conference. The leading economic powers discuss ways of encouraging growth in developing countries.

25

# THE AMERICAN CENTURY

One country towered above all others in the 20th century. It was the richest and most powerful in the world. Its inventors came up with thousands of brilliant ideas, its businesses set new standards, and its athletes were triumphant. Where it went, others followed, copying its language and its lifestyle. The country was, of course, the United States of America.

## DREAM AND NIGHTMARE

▼ Happiness is American bubble gum. In the second half of the century American influence swept around the world in a wave of bubble gum (here blown by a Thai apprentice monk), jeans, and hamburgers.

In the early 1900s about a million people a year, mostly from Europe, were going to live in the United States. They wanted to share in the "American Dream" of riches and freedom. The United States was turning out 30 percent of the world's manufactured goods. Theodore Roosevelt, the soldier, rancher, big-game hunter, explorer, and politician who became president in 1901, captured the country's lively mood.

U.S. business did well out of World War I. Led by the automobile industry, the good times continued into the 1920s. Mighty skyscrapers were symbols of America's confidence and wealth. Although Prohibition (a ban on alcohol) failed and crime increased, things seemed to be getting better and better. The bubble burst in 1929. The Great Depression of the 1930s turned the American Dream into a nightmare. Farming and businesses collapsed, millions lost their jobs. President Franklin D. Roosevelt introduced a New Deal to get the country moving again. It took the edge off people's misery by providing money for jobs and loans for farmers. Even so, the United States did not get fully back to work until World War II.

▲ The all-action president, Theodore Roosevelt, drives a steam crane during the excavation of the Panama Canal, 1906.

## THE GOLDEN AGE

The years after World War II were a golden age for America. Its wealth grew and grew. In 1972 U.S. wages were double those of Japan. Sixty percent of all important inventions were American (1945–60). American films and music entertained the world. The government also tried to make society fairer for women and nonwhites. The crowning glory came in 1969, when millions of TV viewers saw astronaut Neil Armstrong walk on the Moon.

Then, in the 1970s, America suffered three shocks. It lost the unpopular war in Vietnam; a sudden rise in oil prices angered motorists and set back industry; and President Nixon was forced to resign for misusing his powers. In the 1980s President Ronald Reagan got Americans believing in themselves again. Soon the country was as confident as ever. Meanwhile, society was changing fast as the number of Americans from non-European backgrounds grew.

▲ America under a cloud. Gigantic dust storms were one of many serious problems faced by the U.S. during the 1930s.

## THE WORLD'S POLICEMAN

Americans thought of their country as the New World, a place of hope and improvement. Until 1941 they kept their distance from what was happening outside the American continent. They did not try to build up a large overseas empire and joined World War I reluctantly. When it was over, they refused to join the League of Nations.

The Japanese attack on Pearl Harbor (1941) and the United States' enormous effort in World War II changed people's attitudes. The United States was now by far the strongest democratic country and was not prepared to stand and watch the communist USSR and China take over the rest of the world. It poured money into Western Europe, policed Japan, and kept up huge armed forces. It fought communists in Korea and Vietnam, and in the Cuban Missile Crisis (1962) came close to war with the USSR itself. Finally, when communism collapsed, it became a sort of "world policeman." In 1998 its armed forces equaled those of all other major countries combined.

▼ The public face of the United States, represented by smiling Mickey Mouse, sometimes hid the tougher side of the "world's policeman."

## JEANS AND CHEWING GUM

The United States' power grew out of its wealth. For much of the century its banks, businesses, and trade were an engine that pulled the rest of the world. When they crashed in 1929, the whole non-communist world came off the rails. And when the United States did well after World War II, all industrial nations benefited.

TV, books, magazines, and Hollywood films spread the American way of life far and wide. From central Africa to remote Siberia people dressed in jeans and chewed gum. American jumbo jets roared across the skies. Children played with Frisbees and on skateboards and roller blades. There seemed no end to America's influence and amazing creativity.

# THE FIGHT AGAINST RACISM

"I have a dream," said Martin Luther King in 1963, "that one day…the sons of former slaves and the sons of former slave-owners will be able to sit down together at the table of brotherhood." King was an African American who wanted all people to be treated equally. His famous words became the battle cry of one of the 20th century's toughest struggles—the fight against racism.

## THE CAUSES OF RACISM

Racism has existed throughout history. It means judging people by their race, not by the sort of person they are. This can happen for several reasons.

People may fear those of a different race because they look different or follow different customs. They may be jealous of races that seem richer or more skilful than their own. Or, like many 19th-century Europeans, they may think themselves superior to races they have power over. Whatever the cause, racism leads to cruel injustice.

▲ A United Nations soldier protects Sarajevo school-children from the violence of the racist civil war that tore Yugoslavia apart in the early 1990s.

## THE IMPORTANCE OF RACISM

Three changes made racism very important in modern times. First, large numbers of people moved from one country to another, leading to more mixed-race communities. This happened in Britain and France when they accepted settlers from lands that had once been their colonies.

Second, following World War I and the breakup of colonial empires, dozens of new countries appeared. Several contained people of different races and cultures. Yugoslavia, for example, was made up of Serbs, Croats, and Slovenes.

Finally, racists found terrifying new ways of putting their ideas into practice. The machine gun and the gas chamber made it possible for them to wipe out hated minorities completely.

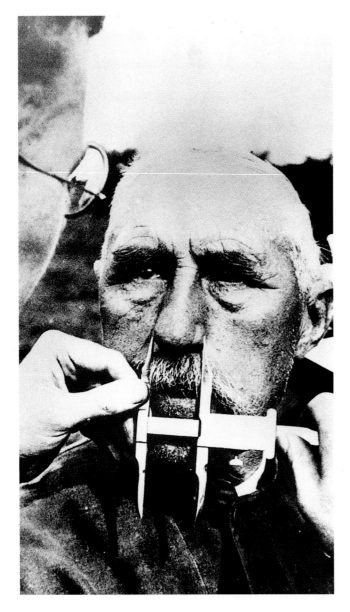

▶ What race do you belong to? A Nazi measures the nose size of a German suspected of coming from a Jewish family. (Jews, who had been mistreated in Europe for centuries, were said to have bigger noses than other people.) This sort of behavior showed how unjust and ridiculous racist policies were.

► Refugees from racism. Tutsi children, driven from their homes by civil war, play in Niashishi refugee camp, Rwanda, 1994.

## TACKLING RACISM

The spread of democracy and human rights helped tackle racism. All citizens of democratic countries, whatever their race, were supposed to have equal rights. To make sure that racial minorities were treated fairly, many governments made racism a crime.

Schools and colleges educated students in non-racist ways. In some Western countries, where racial minorities found it hard to get good jobs, employers kept important posts specially for them. White TV viewers got used to seeing nonwhite actors and presenters.

The fight against racism was not just a matter of right and wrong. When citizens of different races did not get along, law and order could collapse. The United States learned this during the inner-city race riots of the 1960s.

◄ Kathy Freeman, world 400-meter champion in 1997, celebrates her victory by proudly carrying the flag of the Aborigines beside that of Australia.

## ⊙ FIGHT AGAINST RACISM

**1909** Armenians massacred by Turks and Kurds. The racial violence is repeated several times later in the century.

**1912** African National Congress set up to defend black Africans' rights.

**1925–26** Nazi leader Adolf Hitler publishes *Mein Kampf*. The book sets out his hatred of the Jewish race.

**1942** The Nazis begin their "Final Solution." This is the systematic killing of all Jews living in areas under their control.

**1948** The state of Israel founded. The move begins years of conflict between Jews and Arabs.

The government of South Africa begins its racist apartheid policy. It gives blacks no political rights and little share in the country's wealth.

**1955–56** African Americans refuse to use the segregated buses in the state of Alabama.

**1957** U.S. President Eisenhower sends troops to Little Rock, Arkansas. They make sure that children of all races can attend the same school.

**1960** Police fire on peaceful African demonstrators in Sharpeville, South Africa. 69 are killed and 186 wounded.

**1964** South African civil rights leader Nelson Mandela sentenced to life imprisonment. He is released in 1990 and voted South African president in 1994.

Britain bans racial discrimination in hotels and public places. Many other countries pass similar laws.

**1965–68** Race riots rock many U.S. cities.

**1973** The United Nations launches an Anti-Racism Decade. Every country in the UN agrees to support the campaign.

**1975–79** The Cambodian dictator Pol Pot launches a racist holocaust. At least 1 million people die as a result.

**1991–95** Serbs follow racist policy of "ethnic cleansing." The policy aims to get rid of all non-Serbs in Bosnia and Croatia.

**1992** Race riots in Los Angeles.

**1994** Multiracial elections in South Africa.

**1994–96** Millions die in Rwanda's racial civil war.

## A LASTING EVIL

Wartime governments sometimes encouraged racism by labeling the enemy "inferior" or "barbaric." This sort of talk poisoned people's minds for generations. Nation-building also led to racism. Adolf Hitler tried to "purify" his Nazi state by killing millions of Jews. Similarly, in the mid-1990s the Hutu and Tutsi peoples of Rwanda slaughtered each other to get their country for themselves.

# THE YOUNG ONES

Middle-aged men ran the world during the first half of the 20th century. The young had little say in what went on. Graying leaders twice took the world to war, but it was largely young people who were killed. No one under the age of 21 could vote. Most were poorly paid and educated and, particularly in the 1930s, jobs were scarce.

As populations rose after World War II, so did the number of young people. In the wealthier countries they had money in their pockets—money for clothes, radios, records, and even cars and vacations. They felt important and wanted a greater say in politics. By the 1960s they were setting the pace and the older generations struggled to keep up.

▲ "Punk" began as a rebellion against the values of the 1970s but soon became merely a fashion statement.

## THE CULTURE OF YOUTH

Young people began to look different. In the 1920s fashion was largely for the well-off. Now it was for everyone. Styles changed rapidly, from Beat to Hippie to Punk and Grunge. Skirt lengths rose to mini in the 1960s, then plunged down to maxi. Fashionable young men wore their hair long in the 1960s, spiked it in the 1980s, and shaved it off in the 1990s.

The young set the trends for dress—in the 1980s even U.S. President Reagan appeared in jeans. Western bands such as the Beatles wore Oriental patterns and designs. In contrast, Western-style suits became almost a uniform for business people everywhere.

The young behaved differently, too. They wanted to "do their own thing" and had the money and confidence to do it. Beginning with the "angry young men" of the 1950s, they turned their backs on the past. They had fresh ideas about a whole range of issues, such as race, gender, corporal punishment, war, drugs, sex, and marriage.

As a result, the world became less formal and perhaps fairer, too. But with so many traditions and customs gone, it was more confusing. Young people from poor or difficult backgrounds found it hard to cope. They lost hope and turned to vandalism, crime, and drugs.

▶ Although the "swinging sixties" rocked to the music of the Liverpool-born Beatles (Ringo Starr, John Lennon, Paul McCartney, and George Harrison), old men still held power in China, the USSR, and the Vatican.

# ▶ THE YOUNG ONES

**1907** Baden Powell begins the Scouting movement.

**1911** Nursery school opens in London, England.

**1914–18** About 10 million people, mostly young men, die in World War I.

**1918** Russia's communist government proposes free and compulsory school education.

**1925** Egypt introduces free and compulsory education for young children.

**1926** Hitler Youth established.

**1934** Six-year-old Shirley Temple stars in film *Little Miss Marker*.

**1939–45** About 50 million people, many of them under the age of 25, die in World War II.

**1946** Dr. Benjamin Spock publishes *Common Sense Book of Baby and Child Care*. The book sells over 30 million copies and plays an important role in making parents more child-centered.

**1955** Jeans become fashionable.

**1961** John F. Kennedy president of the United States. The election of America's youngest-ever president gives hope to young people everywhere.

**1965** Miniskirts in fashion. Their design shocks many older people.

**1966–67** Red Guards active in China.

**1967** Hippie movement at its height in the "Summer of Love."

**1968** Students riot in Paris. Major protests by young Americans against the Vietnam War.

**1971** U.S. voting age lowered to 18.

**1975** Sneakers becoming fashion garments.

**1977** Rebel "punk" style in fashion.

**1982** United Nations aims to rid Africa of illiteracy by the end of the century.

**1989** About 1000 young protesters killed by security forces in Tiananmen Square, Beijing, China. Most of those who died were calling for democratic rights.

▶ Actor Marlon Brando and his motorcycle in the movie *The Wild One* (1953)—a symbol of youthful rebellion.

▶ "Bright young things"—fashionable young women of the 1920s. They shocked the older generation as much as the "angry young men" of the 50s.

## SCHOOL AND WORK

At the beginning of the century only a small fraction of the world's population could read and write. Fifty years later basic education was seen as a human right and huge strides had been taken towards wiping out illiteracy. By the end of the century about half of all young people in the richer countries enjoyed some form of education after the age of 18.

Well-educated young people were better able to cope with new ideas and technology at work. As a result, the average age of bosses and managers fell. By the 1970s millions of young people working in sports, the media, and business were earning salaries their parents could only dream of. People over the age of 40 were thought too old for many jobs.

## CAMPAIGNS AND PROTEST

Young people played a vital part in 20th-century politics. To get them on their side, in 1926 the Nazis set up the Hitler Youth. Thirteen years later it had almost 9 million members. In 1966 China's Mao Zedong also used the power of youth when he called on Red Guards to lead a Cultural Revolution against his opponents.

Elsewhere, the young rebelled against their governments. Protest reached its height in the 1960s. There were anti-Vietnam War demonstrations in the United States and anti-U.S. demonstrations in Tokyo, Japan. Many countries lowered the voting age to 18.

In the West political protest died down in the 1980s. Caring young people switched their attention to environmental matters, such as pollution and rainforest destruction. Elsewhere, in China for example, the young kept up their demands for human rights and justice.

# TRACK AND FIELD

Sports were already big business by 1914. Over the next 75 years they grew into a multi-billion-dollar global industry. Spectators in the stands or watching on TV could not get enough. Their heroes and heroines, many from humble backgrounds, were household names. Sports often became tangled with politics. International competitions were sometimes used by governments to make political points.

## THE POWER OF MONEY

Modern sports, with their clear rules and standards, began in the all-male private schools of 19th-century Britain. This produced two problems. First, sportswomen found it hard to be taken seriously. Until the 1960s tennis players were the only female athletes to get much media attention. Second, many sports remained amateur—those who took part were not paid. This did not matter to the wealthy, who had time to spare. But it limited the chances of working-class youngsters and those from poorer countries. Professional (paid) athletes did not take part openly in the Olympic Games until 1988.

Soccer, American football, baseball, and golf led the move towards professionalism. Other sports followed, often slowly—Rugby Union in Britain remained amateur until the 1990s. In the end, though, money was all-powerful: American TV rights for the 1976 Olympics cost $25 million; the 1984 rights cost $360 million. By the end of the century sports was the most popular—and expensive—drama in the world.

Television had the power to make or break a sport. Traditional games that looked good on TV, such as all types of football, drew still more money and followers. Other sports, like cricket and rugby, changed their rules and style of play to appeal to the cameras. Sports less easily televised, like sailing, rarely made the headlines.

◀ Jumping for gold: long jumper Jackie Joyner-Kersee at the 1996 Olympic Games in Atlanta. By the end of the century, top track and field athletes were making millions by appearing at major events and endorsing sports equipment.

## NATION AGAINST NATION

International athletic matches began in the British Isles. The first international competition to grab the world's attention was the 1936 Berlin Olympics. Hitler's Nazis planned to use the carefully organized Games to show that the Germans were better than all other peoples. The great African-American sprinter Jesse Owens shattered Nazi dreams by winning four gold medals.

Since then, politicians have often used international sports to get across their message. In 1945 Japan was at war with the United States and its allies. Nineteen years later the Olympics were held in Tokyo, Japan. This showed the world that the war was a thing of the past. Arabs cut sporting links with Israel because of their political differences. When the South African government refused to treat its nonwhite citizens fairly, other countries banned South Africa from international competitions.

▼ Formula 1 driver Jacques Villeneuve in his 1998 Williams car. By the 1990s many governments were challenging the wisdom of allowing tobacco companies to sponsor sporting events because of the link between smoking and ill health.

The Olympic cities map showing: Montreal, Los Angeles, Atlanta, Mexico City, Amsterdam, Antwerp, Stockholm, Helsinki, Moscow, London, Munich, Paris, Rome, Barcelona, Athens, Seoul, Tokyo, Sydney, Melbourne

○ Olympic city

◉ city hosting Olympics more than once

## ▶ TRACK AND FIELD

**1900** Second modern Olympic Games, Paris. The modern Olympic movement began in Athens in 1896.

**1902** American football teams play for the Rose Bowl.

**1903** First Tour de France bicycle race held.

Boston Red Sox win baseball World Series.

**1904** FIFA (Fédération Internationale de Football Association) founded.

**1906** Le Mans, France, hosts 24-hour auto racing Grand Prix.

**1908** African American Jack Johnson becomes world heavyweight boxing champion.

**1912** International Lawn Tennis Federation founded.

**1924** Chamonix, France, hosts first Winter Olympics.

**1927** British and American golfers first play for the Ryder Cup.

**1928** Women's athletics first included in Amsterdam Olympics.

**1930** Uruguay wins soccer World Cup.

**1936** Jesse Owens wins four gold medals in Berlin Olympics.

**1953** Len Hutton becomes first professional English cricket captain.

**1958** Pelé plays in Brazil's first soccer World Cup victory. In 1970 the trophy is given to Brazil, which has won it three times.

**1964** Cassius Clay (Mohammed Ali) becomes world heavyweight boxing champion.

South Africa banned from Olympics (readmitted 1991).

**1972** Arab terrorists attack Olympic village, Munich.

**1976** Many African countries boycott Montreal Olympics to protest the presence of New Zealand, which retained sporting links with South Africa.

**1980** U.S. boycotts Moscow Olympics in protest of the USSR's invasion of Afghanistan. In 1984 communist Europe boycotts the Los Angeles Olympics.

**1987** New Zealands win first Rugby World Cup.

**1994** Colombian footballer Andrés Escobares is murdered because he scored an own goal in his country's defeat in the World Cup.

▲ The Olympic cities, 1896–2000. Neither Africa nor South America hosted the Games in the 20th century.

| | | |
|---|---|---|
| 1896 Athens, Greece | 1932 Los Angeles, USA | 1972 Munich, West Germany |
| 1900 Paris, France | 1936 Munich, Germany | 1976 Montreal, Canada |
| 1904 Los Angeles, USA | 1948 London, Britain | 1980 Moscow, USSR |
| 1908 London, Britain | 1952 Helsinki, Finland | 1984 Los Angeles, USA |
| 1912 Stockholm, Sweden | 1956 Melbourne, Australia | 1988 Seoul, South Korea |
| 1920 Antwerp, Belgium | 1960 Rome, Italy | 1992 Barcelona, Spain |
| 1924 Paris, France | 1964 Tokyo, Japan | 1996 Atlanta, USA |
| 1928 Amsterdam, Netherlands | 1968 Mexico City, Mexico | 2000 Sydney, Australia |

## SPORTS AND SOCIETY

Most citizens of poorer countries, particularly women, had little chance to take part in organized sports. Yet athletic success was one of the few ways they could change their lives. The wish to escape poverty made stars of dozens of Caribbean cricketers, Chinese and Kenyan runners, African-American boxers, and South American soccer players. A handful—Michael Jordan, Pelé, and Mohammed Ali, for example—became legends in their own lifetimes.

The search for success brought problems. Athletes tried to improve their performance with drugs. Men pretended to be women. Bribery and corruption were a serious worry. Supporters, particularly at soccer matches, could become violent. In 1985 the hooliganism of British fans led to 41 deaths in Brussels' Heysel Stadium. Afterwards, European soccer organizations banned British clubs from their competitions.

Sports were not just played by the few and watched by the many. Millions joined in local competitions, and the popularity of non-team games grew. Those who could afford it took part in winter sports and indoor pursuits like squash. Others simply jogged to keep fit. By the 1990s, people living in the industrial nations were obsessed with fitness. Sports shops made fortunes selling expensive gadgets to tone up the flabby bodies of office workers.

Success in sports changed a country's mood and what other people thought of it. The communist government of East Germany helped its sportsmen and women perform wonders from the 1950s to the 1980s. This helped win respect for their country. Politicians and athletes wanted the honor of putting on major sporting events. African states complained because, apart from the 1995 Rugby World Cup, no major international games were held on their continent.

▶ Go team! British police move in to restrain a violent soccer supporter, 1991.

# MAKING SENSE OF IT ALL

The 20th century was a time of fads and fashions, crazes and campaigns. Change was all the rage—what was new one day was "old hat" the next. And it was not just things like clothes and cars that went quickly out of date. Time-honored lifestyles, traditions, and religious faiths were attacked, too. This confused and unsettled some people. Was there anything solid or lasting to hold on to?

## RELIGION UNDER THREAT

Religion was severely shaken up during the 20th century. Sometimes science and religious teachings seemed to contradict each other. Most religions, Christianity and Islam for example, taught that God created the world and everything in it. From the middle of the 19th century scientists were saying this was not true. Human beings had evolved from simple forms of life. A century later they said Earth had not been created either, but had resulted from a "Big Bang" that started the universe.

Communists also criticized religion. They said priests taught the poor about heaven to stop them from thinking about how unfair life was on Earth. Elderly religious leaders did not help themselves, either, when they criticized youth culture or opposed changes like votes for women and the use of birth control.

As a result, in several parts of the world (particularly western Europe and communist countries) old-style religion became less important. Elsewhere it remained as powerful as ever. It inspired people such as Mother Theresa to devote their lives to helping the sick. Archbishop Janani Luwum of Uganda and others sacrificed their lives to support ordinary people against tyranny.

▲ Maharishi Mahesh Yogi discusses Asian religion with Beatles George Harrison and John Lennon, 1967.

## OLD RELIGIONS IN A NEW WORLD

As the world changed, some religious groups changed with it. Others held tight to the past. Many Christian churches brought themselves up-to-date by changing the language of their services and playing jazzy music. Most Protestants accepted women as priests. The United States led the way in changes of this sort and religion there remained very popular.

► Chinese Red Guards reading Mao Zedong's *Little Red Book*. To millions of Chinese, communism was a sort of religion.

▼ Return to God. The last quarter of the century saw a revival of Islam as an alternative to the godless, getting-and-spending culture of the West.

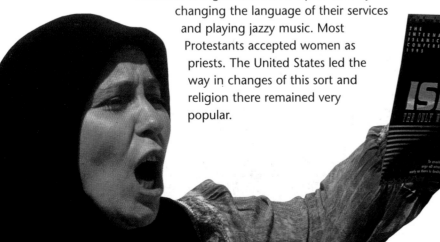

Muslims were less keen on changing. By the end of the century some were fighting back against the modern world. Their leaders urged believers to turn their backs on the corrupt ways of the West and follow the strict word of God as set out in the Koran. In countries such as Saudi Arabia and Afghanistan that accepted this sort of back-to-basics teaching, women were not permitted to show their bodies in public and sinners were executed. The government of Iran even banned satellite dishes so that people could not watch wicked Western TV programs.

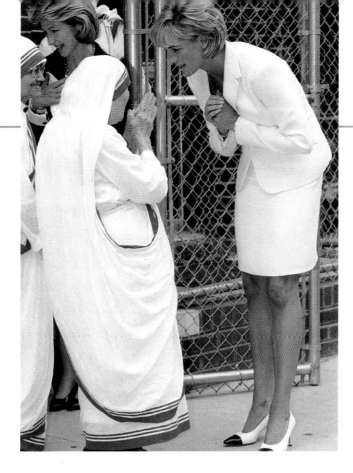

► The meeting of two famous charity workers, 1997. Princess Diana bows before the Catholic nun Mother Theresa of Calcutta.

## ALTERNATIVES

Where people did not have strong religious beliefs, they found other things to believe in. Dictators, like Hitler and Stalin, became godlike figures. Crowds clamored to meet them. Their pictures were widely displayed and their every word praised. For a time the *Little Red Book* of the sayings of Mao Zedong became a sort of bible for young people in China.

Sport became a kind of religion, too. Stadiums were like cathedrals where fans could worship their heroes. The same sort of praise was heaped on stars of stage and screen. When Diana, Princess of Wales, was killed in a car crash in 1997, much of the world mourned as if a saint had died.

Some people in the West looked for happiness in strange ways. They went on spending sprees, took drugs, or got drunk. Others joined weird sects or became obsessed with keeping fit or collecting things. Millions, however, were content not to think about religion too much. But at key moments in their lives, such as weddings and funerals, they flocked back to the churches in millions.

## FAMILY LIFE

Traditional thinking changed most in the richer, industrial countries. At the beginning of the century the normal family consisted of a mother and father living together (even if they disliked each other) with their children. Several generations often shared the same house. Divorce was rare and an unmarried woman who had a baby was considered to be a sinner.

It was very different 100 years later. Many more marriages broke up, couples often lived together outside marriage, and it was quite common for single women to have babies. Critics warned that this sort of behavior led to selfishness and misery. Supporters of the new lifestyle said it grew out of tolerance and understanding, and the old ways only made people guilty and unhappy.

## ► MAKING SENSE OF IT ALL

**1901** Riots in Athens when the church plans to translate the Bible into modern Greek.

**1906** Pentecostal Church set up in U.S.

**1907** Pope condemns many aspects of the modern world. In 1913 he bans religious films.

**1918** All education made non-religious in Russia.

**1928** Islam no longer the official religion of Turkey.

**1930** Pope declares birth control a sin.

Rastafarians say Emperor Haile Selassie of Ethiopia is the living god.

**1931** U.S. religious sect calls itself Jehovah's Witnesses.

**1934** German priests condemn the Nazis.

**1947** Pakistan set up as a separate country for Indian Muslims.

**1950** Buddhist leader, the Dalai Lama, leaves Tibet to escape the communists.

**1953** Church of Scientology set up in U.S.

**1954** Pope says TV a threat to family life.

**1958** Church of England supports family planning.

**1966** Mao Zedong's *Little Red Book* published.

**1970** New English Bible sells 1 million copies in its first day.

**1975** Lebanese civil war starts between Christians and Muslims.

**1977** Archbishop Janani Luwum killed by the forces of Ugandan dictator Idi Amin.

**1978** Mass suicide of The People's Temple cult in Guyana.

**1979** Mother Theresa of Calcutta given the Nobel Peace Prize.

**1983** Polish Pope John Paul II visits his homeland and backs the anti-communist trade union Solidarity.

**1989** First woman bishop.

Ayatollah Khomeini of Iran condemns Salman Rushdie to death. His book *Satanic Verses* is said to be an attack on Islam.

**1995** Iran bans TV satellite dishes.

▼ Practical religion. Christian charities like the Red Cross spent as much time caring for shattered bodies as for shattered souls, particularly in wartime.

35

# CARE AND COOPERATION

Our attention is easily caught by the darker aspects of the 20th century—its wars, famines, and horrible cruelties. But these make up only part of the picture. There were also great improvements in the way individuals were normally treated.

Many countries accepted that all citizens had basic rights. These included the right to choose their government (democracy) and the right to a fair trial if they were accused of doing something wrong. Although these rights were often ignored, it was generally agreed that people ought to have them. Nations learned to co-operate better, too. This was done through organizations such as the United Nations, the European Union, and the Association of Southeast Asian Nations.

## TOWARDS A UNITED EUROPE

In 1900 Europe was a divided continent. In the west stood countries moving towards democracy, including Britain, France, and the Scandinavian states. Old-style empires still ruled much of central and eastern Europe, but these collapsed after World War I. They were replaced by smaller states, such as Poland and Czechoslovakia. Several of them hoped to become democracies.

Sadly, the Great Depression, fascism, and war shattered these high hopes. After World War II Europe was once again divided. The communist USSR controlled the East, where governments took little notice of human rights. But apart from Spain and Portugal, the nations of the West were now democracies. To avoid further war and resist communism, they were determined to build a new Europe.

The first important step was setting up the European Economic Community (1957). This grew into the 15-member European Union, with its own parliament and, eventually, its own bank and currency. After the breakup of the USSR, democracy moved east. The new democracies of eastern Europe were eager to join the Union. By the 1990s, people who had fought each other for centuries were gradually learning the benefits of working together.

▼ Everyone's opinion counts. An Indian woman casts her vote in the Indian elections for a new parliament, 1996. More than 200 million people were eligible to vote.

▲ The right to protest. A single Chinese citizen stands before tanks sent to break up pro-democracy protests in Beijing, 1989. The tanks swerved around him and continued with their brutal task.

## THE ADVANCE OF DEMOCRACY

New Zealand was the first democracy for both men and women (1893). Others countries followed its example, slowly and sometimes unwillingly, over the following 100 years. By the end of the 20th century China was the only major power that did not give its citizens a free vote in elections.

India became the world's most populous democracy in 1947. In the same year Japan brought back free elections. By the 1960s most Western industrial nations were democracies, with votes for women and minority groups. Russia and the nations of eastern Europe followed suit in the early 1990s, and South Africa in 1994.

# ► CARE AND COOPERATION

**1905** Russia elects its duma (parliament). Abolished by the communists, it is reestablished in 1993.

**1910** Portugal becomes a democratic republic.

**1919** League of Nations set up in Geneva, Switzerland.

**1922** International Court of Justice set up at the Hague, Netherlands.

**1928** Kellog–Briand Pact signed by 15 nations. The Pact renounces war as a way of settling disputes.

**1931** Commonwealth of Nations set up. It is joined by over 70 countries, all of which were once part of the British Empire.

**1933** Japan leaves the League of Nations. The League had condemned Japan's occupation of Manchuria, China.

World Economic Conference held. It fails to agree how to tackle the Great Depression.

**1935–36** Italy ignores the League of Nations and invades Abyssinia.

**1945** United Nations is established.

**1947** Japan becomes a democracy.

GATT (General Agreement on Trade and Tariffs) established to regulate world trade.

**1950** European Coal and Steel Community set up. It becomes the European Economic Community in the 1956 Treaty of Rome.

India declared a democratic republic.

**1955** Geneva summit meeting held to ease East–West relations.

**1961** Amnesty International is set up to campaign on behalf of political prisoners.

**1967** Association of South East Asian Nations (ASEAN) is established to promote political, economic, and social cooperation. In 1989 it joins with other Pacific Rim countries to become the Council for Asia–Pacific Economic Cooperation.

**1973** Britain joins the EEC.

**1975** Helsinki agreement. 35 nations agree to freeze frontiers, renounce force, and work for human rights.

**1982** Free elections reestablished in Brazil.

**1987** Free elections reestablished in Turkey.

**1989** Democracy reemerging in Russia, Poland, Czechoslovakia, and other east European states.

**1991** Maastricht Treaty establishes European Union.

**1995** South American countries set up Southern Common Market (Mercosur).

**1997** China's leadership apologizes for the brutal treatment of pro-democracy demonstrators in Beijing's Tiananamen Square (1989).

▲ The first meeting of the Council of the League of Nations, 1919. The League could not get countries to obey its decisions and was largely ignored after 1936.

## WORKING TOGETHER

Following the horrifying slaughter of World War I, 45 states set up the League of Nations. It aimed to prevent future conflicts and encourage nations to work more closely together. Although the League was a noble idea, the United States did not join. The League was powerless to stop Japan, Italy, Germany, and the USSR from attacking weaker countries.

After World War II the much stronger United Nations (UN) replaced the League of Nations. All the major powers joined. Guided by its Security Council and General Assembly, it sent out its own peacekeeping forces. It also worked through helpful international organizations. These included the World Bank, the World Health Organization, and the Economic and Social Council, which looked at issues like human rights, poverty, and the drug trade.

The UN was nothing like a world government, and it usually spent more time talking than acting. But at least it brought people together to discuss their problems and differences. This was also done at a growing number of international meetings and conferences. Their subjects ranged from arms control to the environment. Never before had human beings struggled so hard to cooperate.

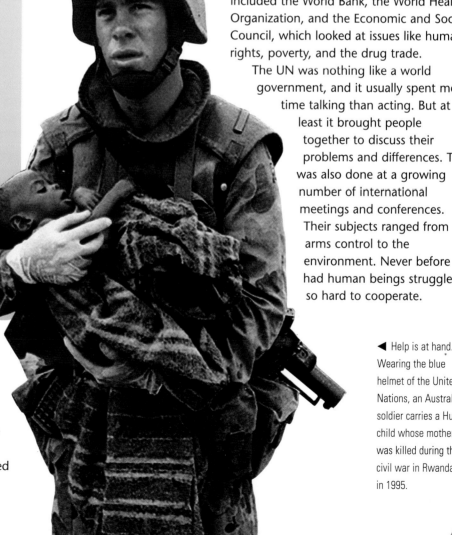

Democracy found it harder to take root in the rest of Africa and the Arab world. In Nigeria, for example, Africa's most populous country, the British style of government set up in 1960 soon collapsed. Tribal differences tore the country apart, and the army got rid of governments it did not like. There were similar problems in Central and South America. Nevertheless, by 1995 both Brazil and Argentina enjoyed democratic government.

◄ Help is at hand. Wearing the blue helmet of the United Nations, an Australian soldier carries a Hutu child whose mother was killed during the civil war in Rwanda in 1995.

# THE SHRINKING WORLD

In October 1962 the United States and the USSR came terrifyingly close to nuclear war. Ten months later an emergency "hot line" was opened between the offices of the U.S. president and the Soviet head of state. The link allowed the leaders of the two superpowers to contact each other directly in times of crisis. It was one of the most dramatic examples of how communications improved during the 20th century.

## WIRELESS

The foundations of modern electronic communications were laid in the 19th century, when the telegraph and the telephone were invented. These enabled messages to be sent quickly and reliably over long distances. The next major step forward was discovering how to send signals, then words and pictures, through the air without the need for wires.

The process developed in two stages. Very early in the century scientists managed to transmit radio signals thousands of miles and use them to send speech and pictures. This led to the first radio broadcasts and radio telephones. By the late 1920s moving pictures could be transmitted, paving the way for early television broadcasts in the 1930s.

The second wave of development was based around two inventions: the transistor and the microchip. Together with space technology, they began the age of telecommunication. Radios, televisions, and telephones became smaller, portable, and cheaper. Satellites and receiver dishes allowed programs to be broadcast over the five continents. Finally, the computer-based Internet made it possible to link every home and workplace to a worldwide web of instant information.

▲ The Irish-Italian wireless pioneer Guglielmo Marconi was the first person to send a radio signal across the Atlantic. He became a wealthy businessman and a strong supporter of fascism.

## HERE IS THE NEWS

At the beginning of the century newspapers were the chief means of passing on the news and up-to-date information. Reporters sent in their stories by letter or telegram. Readers found out what was going on around the world sometimes days after it had happened. Most pictures were hand-drawn.

By the 1940s the radio was generally first with the news. Thirty years later TV flashed the latest stories around the world in words and moving color pictures. By the end of the century there were TV stations that handled only news and the Internet gave even more details. Deaths, disasters, sports triumphs, and discoveries were known everywhere the moment they happened. It was as if the world had become a huge village in which everyone knew immediately what everyone else was doing.

In the early years of the century newspaper owners had great influence. They decided what was news and how it would be handled. By the 1960s much of this power had passed to those who managed TV and radio stations. A good example of the power of TV occurred during the Vietnam War. American TV journalists covered the war in great depth. When the viewers at home saw the horrifying things that were going on, they turned against the slaughter. Partly as a result of this, the United States was forced to pull out of the war.

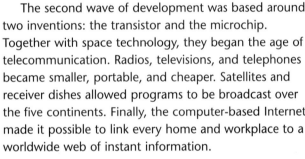

▼ A communication satellite orbiting high above the Earth. Satellites like this can relay TV programs, telephone conversations, faxes, and emails across the world in seconds.

# ▶ THE SHRINKING WORLD

**1900** R. A. Fessenden transmits speech by radio.

**1901** Guglielmo Marconi sends first transatlantic radio message.

**1904** The German Arthur Korn sends first pictures by wireless telegraph.

**1906** R. A. Fessenden makes first radio broadcast.

**1922** British Broadcasting Company (later Corporation) founded.

**1925** "Wireless" radio receivers (with valves) available.

**1926** John Logie Baird demonstrates his television. Regular TV broadcasts begin in the 1930s.

**1938** Photocopier invented.

**1942** Magnetic tape invented.

**1946** First electronic computer built. It is the size of a room.

**1948** Transistor invented.

**1955** U.S. President Eisenhower holds a televised news conference.

**1956** Transatlantic telephone service introduced.

**1958** Xerox Corporation markets first office photocopier.

**1959** Microchip invented.

**1962** Telstar TV satellite launched to relay TV signals across the Atlantic.

**1969** Internet established. It does not expand worldwide until the 1990s.

**1970** Open University set up in Britain
    Floppy disk developed.

**1975** Personal computers (PCs) first on sale.

**1979** TV broadcasts by satellite.

**1980s** Mobile phones and faxes widely available.

**1986** Laptop computers introduced.

As TV grew in importance, so did TV advertising. It attracted many of the best filmmakers, writers, and artists. Those who appeared on TV had to learn how to handle the new means of communication. Politicians, entertainers, and athletes were taught to think carefully about their clothes, their expressions, and every word they spoke. Image became all-important.

◀ Forget the suffering, it's the image that matters. Photographers follow screaming children during the Vietnam War, 1972.

## INFORMATION FOR ALL

The media revolution affected the lives of almost everyone. The pace of life speeded up as telephone conversations, faxes, and emails replaced traditional letters. As newspapers could no longer be first with the news, they became more like illustrated magazines. Schools and universities tuned in to special educational broadcasts. By the 1990s the new communications technology was allowing people to work from home.

Just as they had tried to control books and newspapers, politicians struggled to control the new types of communication. For years the British allowed only the BBC to broadcast programs. But the air waves were extremely difficult to police, and satellite broadcasting and the Internet were almost impossible to control. Anyone with a satellite dish or a computer modem had access to a world of information that would never have been dreamt of 100 years earlier.

▶ The end of isolation. By the 1990s no ambitious young businessperson was complete without a mobile phone.

# SAVING THE EARTH

Throughout the 19th and 20th centuries the world became more and more industrial. The population rose sharply, too. By the middle of the 20th century pollution and damage to the environment were worrying. By the end of the century they were very serious problems indeed. Scientists were warning that human civilization might be destroying itself.

## THE LIMITS OF GROWTH

Until the 1970s people believed that industry and technology could go on steadily advancing. They recognized environmental problems, but thought that these could be dealt with as and when necessary. In this frame of mind, many countries took steps to protect their forests, rivers, and wildlife. They also passed laws to control smoke and other obvious forms of pollution.

By the 1970s scientists were doubting this happy-go-lucky way of looking at things. For example, in their book *The Limits of Growth* (1972), a group of researchers said that industry could not go on churning out ever more products. The Earth could not stand it. If things went on as they were, they warned, there would soon be so many people and so much pollution that life would become horrible for everyone.

Over the next ten years the environment became a topic of great importance. But experts did not agree on two main issues: how serious were man-made changes to the environment? And what could be done to stop things from getting worse?

## THE GREAT DEBATE

▼ One's enough. A poster backing the Chinese government's drive to cut population growth by limiting couples to a single child.

Some changes in the environment were obvious and alarming. The Great Lakes of North America turned into lifeless sewers. Smoke and car exhaust fumes poisoned the air in great cities such as London, Tokyo, and Los Angeles. Acid rain destroyed whole forests in northern Europe. Sea water became unfit for swimming. Hunting and destruction of the natural habitat threatened hundreds of species of plants and animals, most notably whales, tigers, pandas, and elephants. People's attention was caught by terrible disasters, such as the leak of radiation from the Chernobyl nuclear plant and the pollution of the Alaskan coast by oil from the supertanker *Exxon Valdez*.

Many argued that more serious disasters were looming. They were most concerned about "global warming." The massive forests that removed carbon dioxide from the air were being cut down, while at the same time the burning of coal and oil was adding billions more tons of carbon dioxide (and other gases) to the atmosphere. This was putting a thick blanket of gases around the planet. As inside a greenhouse, temperatures were rising. Deserts were getting bigger. In time, if the ice at the North and South Poles melted, coasts could flood and some islands disappear beneath the sea. It was a terrifying prophesy.

▲ A flare-carrier guides a London bus through the city's suffocating smog, 1952.

# ► SAVING THE EARTH

**1906** U.S. sets up National Forests Commission.

**1926** Council for the Protection of Rural England (CPRE) founded.

**1927** Margaret Sanger organizes World Population Conference.

**1929** U.S. Migratory Bird Conservation Act passed.

**1930** World population reaches 2 billion.

**1936** National Wildlife Federation set up in U.S.

**1951** Electricity first generated from nuclear power.

**1955** Clean Air Act in Britain. Air pollution is causing thousands of deaths in large cities.

**1963** Rachel Carson's *Silent Spring* warns of the dangers of chemical pollution.

**1967** "Greenhouse effect" suggested.

**1970** U.S. sets up Environmental Protection Agency.

**1971** Environmental group Greenpeace formed.

**1972** *The Limits of Growth* published. It is one of the first and most important warnings about future environmental disaster.

**1974** World population reaches 4 billion.

Discovery of damage to the atmosphere's ozone layer by CFC gases. A worldwide ban on the production of CFCs follows.

**1977** UN conference held on the spread of the world's deserts.

**1984** 2000 die as a result of chemical leakage in Bhopal, India.

**1986** Soviet nuclear reactor at Chernobyl explodes. Radiation from the world's worst nuclear accident spreads for thousands of miles.

**1989** Worldwide ban on ivory trade established.

*Exxon Valdez* supertanker disaster. The spillage of 17 million gallons of oil causes a major environmental disaster.

**1992** UN Conference on the Environment, Rio de Janeiro. Real concern is shown about environmental damage but there is no firm agreement about what is to be done.

**1997** UN Conference on the Environment held in Kyoto.

World's hottest year since records began.

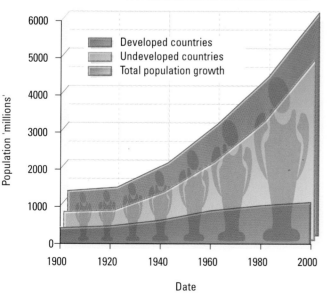

◄ Population growth in the 20th century. World population grew ever more rapidly, especially in developing countries.

◄ Shaving the Earth —destruction of forests and woodlands is perhaps our most serious act of environmental vandalism.

## REACTIONS

The first environmental protection groups, such as the U.S. National Forests Commission, dated from the early part of the century. By the 1990s there were thousands of organizations, ranging from international groups such as Greenpeace to smaller campaigns such as Save the Whales. Some governments listened to people's worries. They made anti-pollution laws stricter and improved public transportation so that drivers did not need to use their cars so much. Cities like Paris occasionally banned some car use altogether.

There were three reasons why more was not done. First, "green" policies, like removing the harmful gases put out by power stations and cars, were very expensive.

Second, not everyone believed things were getting worse. People welcomed action only when they saw that it was necessary. For example, the British passed a Clean Air Act only when they saw for themselves the harmful effects of smoke pollution. It was much harder to get people to use their cars less because no one could prove that exhaust gases caused temperatures to rise.

Finally, serious action on the environment needed countries to act together. This was often possible with local problems, as when European and North African countries agreed to clean up the Mediterranean. But global conferences on the environment in 1992 and 1997 met with serious difficulties. Wealthy nations, such as Australia, did not want to do anything that harmed their prosperity. Less well-off countries, like China, would not cut the amount of harmful gases they produced just to help super-rich countries like the United States. In the end, the 20th century handed on the problem of the environment to future generations.

# TIMELINE

**1900**

R. A. Fessenden transmits speech by radio; the beginning of "wireless" broadcasting.

**1901**
Commonwealth of Australia established. Artist Pablo Picasso moves to Paris, where his talent is soon recognized.

**1902**
Foot-binding banned in China. Ernest Starling and William Bayliss discover the first hormones.

**1903**
The Wright brothers' Flyer makes the first steady flight by a heavier-than-air machine.

**1904**
War breaks out between Russia and Japan (to 1905).

**1905**
Uprisings force Tsar Nicholas II to allow Russia's first elected duma (parliament).

**1906**
Auto racing Grand Prix held at Le Mans, France.

Chinese women get the right to vote.

First supermarket opens in San Francisco.

Insulin injections first given to diabetes sufferers.
Dictator Benito Mussolini takes power in Italy.

Sale of alcohol banned (Prohibition) in U.S. (lasts until 1933).

**1925**
**1924**
**1923**
**1922**
**1921**
**1920**
**1919**

Charleston dance craze sweeps across Western world.

Abstract painter Wassily Kandinsky founds Russian Academy of Artistic Sciences.
Chinese communist party established.

Treaty of Versailles. League of Nations established.

**1926**
Scotsman John Logie Baird first demonstrates television.

**1927**
*The Jazz Singer* is the first "talking film."

**1928**
First Mickey Mouse cartoon film made.
Penicillin discovered.
Stalin in power in Soviet Union.

Cologne–Bonn autobahn (the first highway) opened.
Franklin D. Roosevelt elected president of U.S.

Hitler becomes chancellor of Germany, bringing Nazis to power.
Roosevelt introduces his New Deal.

**1929**
**1930**
**1931**
**1932**
**1933**
**1934**

Wall Street crash begins the Great Depression.

Uruguay wins first soccer World Cup

Empire State Building in New York completed.
Japan seizes Chinese province of Manchuria.
Canada and New Zealand become independent nations.

Nylon invented by U.S. chemist Wallace Carothers.

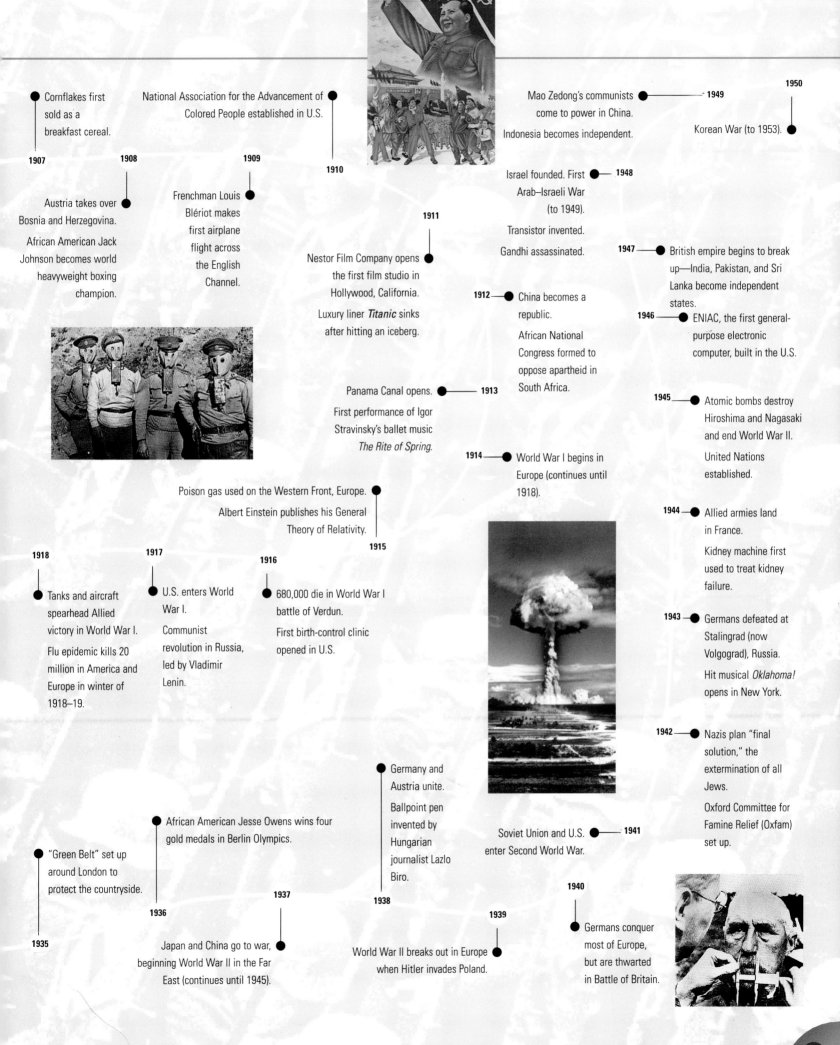

Cornflakes first
sold as a
breakfast cereal.

National Association for the Advancement of
Colored People established in U.S.

**1907**　　**1908**　　　　　　**1909**

Austria takes over
Bosnia and Herzegovina.

African American Jack
Johnson becomes world
heavyweight boxing
champion.

Frenchman Louis
Blériot makes
first airplane
flight across
the English
Channel.

**1910**

**1911**

Nestor Film Company opens
the first film studio in
Hollywood, California.

Luxury liner *Titanic* sinks
after hitting an iceberg.

**1912**　China becomes a
republic.

African National
Congress formed to
oppose apartheid in
South Africa.

Panama Canal opens. ● ─ **1913**

First performance of Igor
Stravinsky's ballet music
*The Rite of Spring*.

**1914** ─ World War I begins in
Europe (continues until
1918).

Poison gas used on the Western Front, Europe. ●

Albert Einstein publishes his General
Theory of Relativity.

**1915**

**1918**　　　　**1917**　　　　　　**1916**

Tanks and aircraft
spearhead Allied
victory in World War I.

Flu epidemic kills 20
million in America and
Europe in winter of
1918–19.

U.S. enters World
War I.

Communist
revolution in Russia,
led by Vladimir
Lenin.

680,000 die in World War I
battle of Verdun.

First birth-control clinic
opened in U.S.

Mao Zedong's communists ● ─ ' **1949**
come to power in China.

Indonesia becomes independent.

**1950**

Korean War (to 1953). ●

Israel founded. First ● ─ **1948**
Arab–Israeli War
(to 1949).

Transistor invented.

Gandhi assassinated.

**1947** ─ ● British empire begins to break
up—India, Pakistan, and Sri
Lanka become independent
states.

**1946** ─ ● ENIAC, the first general-
purpose electronic
computer, built in the U.S.

**1945** ─ ● Atomic bombs destroy
Hiroshima and Nagasaki
and end World War II.

United Nations
established.

**1944** ─ ● Allied armies land
in France.

Kidney machine first
used to treat kidney
failure.

**1943** ─ ● Germans defeated at
Stalingrad (now
Volgograd), Russia.

Hit musical *Oklahoma!*
opens in New York.

**1942** ─ ● Nazis plan "final
solution," the
extermination of all
Jews.

Oxford Committee for
Famine Relief (Oxfam)
set up.

Germany and
Austria unite.

Ballpoint pen
invented by
Hungarian
journalist Lazlo
Biro.

Soviet Union and U.S. ● ─ **1941**
enter Second World War.

African American Jesse Owens wins four
gold medals in Berlin Olympics.

"Green Belt" set up
around London to
protect the countryside.

**1937**

**1936**

**1940**

**1935**

Japan and China go to war, ●
beginning World War II in the Far
East (continues until 1945).

**1938**

**1939**

World War II breaks out in Europe ●
when Hitler invades Poland.

Germans conquer
most of Europe,
but are thwarted
in Battle of Britain.

**1951** Libya becomes independent. Electricity generated from nuclear power.

**1952** First successful sex-change operation.

**1953** Death of Stalin. Nikita Khrushchev's more moderate rule in Soviet Union (to 1964). James Watson and Francis Crick discover DNA, the basic genetic material.

**1954** 19-year-old Elvis Presley makes his first record. France defeated in Vietnam. Pope says TV is a threat to family life.

**1955** First performance of Samuel Beckett's play *Waiting for Godot.*

**1956** Egypt takes over Suez Canal. Soviet Union invades Hungary.

**1957** European Economic Community (now European Union) founded. Ghana and Malaysia become independent. Soviet Union launches man-made satellite, *Sputnik I.*

**1958** Pelé plays in Brazil's first soccer World Cup victory. Xerox introduces the first office photocopier.

**1959** Microchip invented.

**1960** Police kill 67 demonstrators in Sharpeville, South Africa. Sirimavo Bandaranaike becomes the world's first elected woman leader, Ceylon (Sri Lanka).

**1961** Berlin Wall built. Amnesty International established to campaign on behalf of political prisoners.

**1962** Cuban missile crisis brings U.S. and Soviet Union to brink of war. *Telstar* communications satellite sends live TV pictures across the Atlantic.

**1963** President Kennedy assassinated. Rachel Carson's *Silent Spring* warns of the dangers of chemical pollution. Beatles' first hit single "Love Me Do" is released.

**1964** U.S. involved in Vietnam War (until 1975).

**1965** Race riots in many U.S. cities (until 1968). Miniskirts in fashion.

**1966** Mao Zedong launches China's Cultural Revolution.

**1983** Polish Pope John Paul II backs the Polish anti-communist trade union Solidarity.

**1984** 2000 die when poisonous chemicals leak from factory in Bhopal, India.

**1985** Indian prime minister Indira Gandhi assassinated. Laser surgery developed. Mikhail Gorbachev introduces "glasnost" (openness) and "perestroika" (reorganizing) into the Soviet Union.

**1986** Soviet nuclear reactor at Chernobyl explodes. Radioactive dust blows across Europe.

**1987** New Zealand wins Rugby World Cup.

**1988** European Union's "set-aside" policy pays European farmers for not producing food.

**1989** Democracy emerging in Russia, Poland, Czechoslovakia and other eastern European states. Berlin Wall comes down.

**1990** Iraq invades Kuwait and is driven out by the United Nations (1991).

**1991** Civil war in Yugoslavia, which breaks up. Serbs follow racist policy of "ethnic cleansing" (to 1995).

**1992** First CD-ROM computer disks go on sale.

**1993** Military coup ends civilian rule in Nigeria.

**1994** Democratic elections involving all races in South Africa. Nelson Mandela elected president. Channel Tunnel opens between Britain and France.

● Iran's strict Muslim regime bans TV satellite dishes.

**1995**

● Ice discovered on the Moon.

India and Pakistan test nuclear weapons.

**1998**

**1999**

**2000**

**1996**

Russia launches full-scale but unsuccessful attack against Chechnya.

Computer graphics film *Toy Story* released.

**1997**

World's hottest year since records began.

Widespread fires burn rainforests in Indonesia and the Amazon basin.

● European Union introduces a single currency.

● Olympic Games held in Sydney, Australia.

● Mother Theresa of Calcutta awarded the Nobel Peace Prize.

Soviet troops invade Afghanistan.

Muslim revolution in Iran.

**1979**

**1978**

● Israel and Egypt make peace at Camp David.

TV soap opera *Dallas* attracts audiences of many millions.

**1977**

● Pompidou Center opens in Paris.

Punk music and fashion popular in Britain and U.S.

**1982**

● First music CDs go on sale.

**1981**

● TV audience of 700 million watches wedding of Prince Charles and Lady Diana Spencer.

**1980**

● Iran–Iraq War (to 1988).

Smallpox eradicated from Earth.

**1976** ——● Death of Mao Zedong signals beginning of more relaxed regime in China.

Cambodian dictator Pol Pot begins ●—— **1975** racist killings that leave at least 1 million dead by 1979.

World population reaches 4 billion. ●—— **1974**

Discovery of damage to ozone layer by CFC gases.

● Second Arab–Israeli War.

"Greenhouse effect" suggested.

Hippies celebrate "summer of love."

**1967**

● British troops sent to Northern Ireland.

Apollo 11 mission lands on the moon.

**1969**

● Boeing 747 "Jumbo" jet enters service.

**1970**

● General Amin seizes power in Uganda (to 1979).

Environmental group Greenpeace formed.

**1971**

● Anti-Israeli Arabs launch terrorist attack on Olympic village, Munich.

**1972**

**1973** ●—— Third Arab–Israeli War. Cut in Arab oil production causes worldwide economic hardship.

Sydney Opera House opens.

**1968**

● Soviet Union invades Czechoslovakia.

Vaccine for meningitis available.

# GLOSSARY

**antibiotics** Powerful drugs that kill bacteria or fungi.

**apartheid** South Africa's racist policy of "separate development" for black and white peoples. In practice, it meant white supremacy.

**architect** Someone who designs buildings or groups of buildings.

**birth control** Preventing conception ("contraception") to limit the number of children born to a couple.

**campaign** A series of operations with a definite aim, such as a military campaign or the campaign against racism.

**capitalism** The **economic** system in which private businesses are free to compete with each other. It is the opposite of **communism**.

**civil war** War fought within a single country.

**cold war** Open hostility between two sides that stops short of shooting ("hot war").

**colony** An overseas possession in a country's **empire**.

**communism** The political and **economic** system in which everything is owned and controlled by the **state**.

**consumer** Someone who buys goods or services.

**crisis** A key moment; a turning point.

**currency** A country's money, such as the U.S. dollar or the Japanese yen.

**democracy** The political system in which all adult citizens have a say in the government.

**demonstration** An organized protest.

**depression** A serious **economic** downturn, when businesses close and **unemployment** rises.

**dictator** An all-powerful leader.

**economy** The finances, including business and trade, of a country, region, etc. The adjective is **economic**.

**empire** A group of **states**, **colonies**, etc. under the control of a single country.

**fascism** The anti-**communist** system of government set up in Italy in the 1920s and Germany in the 1930s. Fascist **states** were governed by **dictators**.

**feminism** Belief in equal rights and opportunities for women.

**Great Depression** The serious, worldwide economic **recession** that lasted from about 1929 until the later 1930s.

**illegal** Against the law.

**illiterate** Unable to read or write.

**independence** Freedom to govern oneself.

**inoculation** To protect against a disease by giving someone a mild form of that disease.

**media** The means of mass communication, such as newspapers, radio, and TV.

**minority** A group, usually of a distinct race or culture, that is outnumbered by the majority. The Jews, for example, were a minority in Nazi Germany.

**nation** A country that governs itself.

**radiation** The rays given out by substances such as uranium. The radiation from nuclear power plants and explosions is extremely harmful.

**recession** A period of **economic** slowing down or decline.

**republic** A **state** not headed by a king or queen.

**revolution** A quick, total, and permanent change.

**salary** Wages paid by the week, or longer period of time, rather than by the hour.

**state** A country or smaller unit. *The* state is the government.

**suffragettes** Women who **campaigned** for the right to vote.

**telegraph** Messages (but not speech) transmitted by cable.

**terrorist** Someone who **campaigns** by violent means, such as bombing or hijacking.

**trade union** An organization of workers to **campaign** for better pay and conditions.

**unemployment** being out of work.

**vaccine** The substance used in **inoculation**.

**welfare** Government assistance, such as medical care and **unemployment** pay, for the less well-off.

# INDEX

# ACKNOWLEDGEMENTS

**Photos**
*Abbreviations : ET = E.T. Archive; HG = Hulton Getty;*
*SPL = Science Photo Library; TS = Getty Images/Tony Stone.*

Cover SPL; title page  SPL; 3bl Jeremy Horner/TS; 3tr AKG London; 3cr ET; 3br Popperfoto; 4–5(background) Ed Pritchard/TS; 4tl TS; br SPL; 5tl AKG; 5cr Still Pictures/CH Zuber; 5br Rex Features; 6–7 AKG; 6tr Popperfoto; 6bl AKG/Ghandhi Photo Service Bombay–Berlin;  8c Ed Pritchard/TS; 8b HG; 9t J. Young/Telegraph Colour Library; 9b NASA/SPL; 10tr, bl AKG London; 11t ET; 11b Mark Edwards/Still Pictures; 12tr Corinne Dufka/Popperfoto/Reuter; 12bl AKG; 13tr, cr Peter Newark's Military Pictures; 13bl C. H. Zuber/Still Pictures; 14bl HG; 14tr, 15tl AKG; 15br Henning Bock/AKG Berlin; 16(inset) CC Studio/SPL; 16c Deep Light Productions/SPL; 16br Bernard Pierre Wolff/SPL; 17tl Wellcome Institute Library; London; 17br, 18cr Popperfoto; 18bl Scozzari-unep/Still Pictures; 18–19 AKG; 19br AKG/AP; 19tr Sally & Richard Greenhill; 20tr William Sewell/ET; 20bl AKG; 21tr, cr Popperfoto; 21bl AKG London; 22cr HG; 22bl, 23b Popperfoto; 23tl Mark Edwards/Still Pictures; 24t Donna Day/TS; 24b Jim Hollander/Reuter/Corbis UK Ltd; 25tl HG; 25br Popperfoto; 25bl Sue Cunningham/TS; 26bl Jeremy Horner/TS; 26tr Peter Newark's American Pictures; 27tl HG; 27br Rex Features; 27(box) TS; 28tr Popperfoto; 28bl AKG; 29t Pascal Guyot/AFB Photos; 29b Richard Martin/Agence Vandystadt/Allsport; 30cl Sally & Richard Greenhill; 30b AKG

London; 31tr HG; 31b Kobal; 32t Allsport; 32b Gustau Nacarino/Popperfoto/Reuter; 33 Richard Sellers/Sportsphoto Agency; 34tr AKG/AP; 34cr Popperfoto; 34bl Julio Etchart/Still Pictures; 35t Popperfoto/Reuter; 35b Popperfoto; 36tr Popperfoto/Reuter; 36bl Popperfoto/Reuter; 37t HD; 37b Joe Alexander/AFP Photos; 38tr Rex Features; 38bl SPL; 39(box) Corbis–Bettman; 39tr Popperphoto; 39br Hartmut Schwarzbach/Still Pictures; 40tr HG; 40bl Julio Etchart/Still Pictures; 41 Daniel Dancer/Still Pictures; 42–3(background) AKG; 42tl AKG London; 42tr Peter Newark's Military Pictures; 42bl Rex Features; 42br HD; 43tc William Sewell/ET; 43cl, br AKG; 43cr C.H. Zuber/Still Pictures; 44–5(background) TS/Moggy Jeans;  44tr Popperfoto/Bouys; 44cr AKG/AP; 44bl ET ; 45tl Popperfoto/Reuter; 45tc Simon Walker/Rex Features; 45tr Sally & Richard Greenhill; 45bc Bernard Pierre Wolff/SPL; 45br Henning Bock/AKG.

**Artwork**
7t, 33t Olive Pearson; 41b James Sneddon.